BAKHTIN

Rethinking Theory

GENERAL EDITOR

Gary Saul Morson

CONSULTING EDITORS

Robert Alter
Frederick Crews
John M. Ellis
Caryl Emerson

BAKHTIN

Ethics and Mechanics

Edited by

Valerie Z. Nollan

Northwestern University Press
Evanston, Illinois

Northwestern University Press
Evanston, Illinois 60208-4210

Copyright © 2004 by Northwestern University Press.
Published 2004. All rights reserved.

Printed in the United States of America

10 9 8 7 6 5 4 3 2 1

ISBN 0-8101-1671-5 (cloth)
ISBN 0-8101-1515-8 (paper)

Library of Congress Cataloging-in-Publication Data

Bakhtin : ethics and mechanics / edited by Valerie Z. Nollan.
     p. cm. — (Rethinking theory)
   Includes bibliographical references.
    ISBN 0-8101-1671-5 (cloth : alk. paper) — ISBN 0-8101-1515-8
(pbk. : alk. paper)
   1. Bakhtin, M. M. (Mikhail Mikhaĭlovich, 1895–1975—Philosophy.
   2. Literature—Philosophy.   3. Literature—History and criticism—
Theory, etc.   I. Nollan, Valerie Z.   II. Series.
PG2947.B3B334 2003
801'.95'092—dc21   2003009363

The paper used in this publication meets the minimum requirements of the
American National Standard for Information Sciences—Permanence of Paper
for Printed Library Materials, ANSI Z39.48-1992.

For Richard and Alex

Contents

Acknowledgments   ix

List of Abbreviations   xi

Valerie Z. Nollan
Introduction   xiii

David Krasner
Dialogics and Dialectics: Bakhtin, Young Hegelians, and Dramatic Theory   3

Jacqueline A. Zubeck
Bakhtin's Ethics and an Iconographic Standard in *Crime and Punishment*   33

Kimberly A. Nance
Let Us Say That There Is a Human Being before Me Who Is Suffering:
Empathy, Exotopy, and Ethics in the Reception of Latin American
Collaborative *Testimonio*   57

Valerie Z. Nollan
Russia as a Chronotope in Works by Ruralist Writers: Toward a Philosophy
of the Art   75

Contributors   95

Acknowledgments

I would like to express my gratitude to Caryl Emerson, Susan Harris, Gary Saul Morson, and Richard Nollan for their unflagging support of this project; to Brynn Keith, Alexandra Kostina, Kathy Nash, Markus Pott, and Mary Quinlan for their friendship and collegiality; to Tiffany Hart for her technical assistance; to Rhodes College for providing excellent facilities and financial support at various stages of the book; and to my parents, Eugenia and Julian Caseria, for their love and encouragement.

This book could not have been written without the music of Sergei Vasilie-vich Rachmaninoff.

Abbreviations

CP Fyodor Dostoevsky, *Crime and Punishment* [1866]. Translated by Constance Garnett. New York: Bantam Books, 1981.

DI Mikhail Bakhtin, *The Dialogic Imagination: Four Essays by M. M. Bakhtin*. Edited by Michael Holquist. Translated by Caryl Emerson and Michael Holquist. Austin: Univ. of Texas Press, 1981.

Icons Leonid Ouspensky and Vladimir Lossky, *The Meaning of Icons*. Translated by G. E. H. Palmer and E. Kadloubovsky. Boston: Boston Book and Art Shop, Inc., 1969.

"Idea" Mikhail Bakhtin, "The Idea in Dostoevsky," *Problems in Dostoevsky's Poetics*. Edited and translated by Caryl Emerson. Minneapolis: Univ. of Minnesota Press, 1984.

MY Joseph Frank, *Dostoevsky: The Miraculous Years 1865–1871*. Princeton, N.J.: Princeton University Press, 1995.

PDP Mikhail Bakhtin, *Problems of Dostoevsky's Poetics* [1963]. Edited and translated by Caryl Emerson. Minneapolis: Univ. of Minnesota Press, 1984.

TPA Mikhail Bakhtin, *Toward a Philosophy of the Act*. Edited by Michael Holquist and Vadim Liapunov. Translation and notes by Vadim Liapunov. Austin: Univ. of Texas Press, 1993.

Uspensky Boris Uspensky, *The Semiotics of the Russian Icon*. Edited by Stephen Rudy. Translated by P. A. Reed. Lisse: Peter DeRidder Press, 1976.

Introduction

Valerie Z. Nollan

Origins of the Essays

This collection of essays evolved from the seminar "Working with Bakhtin Today" that was hosted by Pennsylvania State University from July 25 to 29, 1995. The seminar consisted of three different workshops, each conducted by a distinguished Bakhtin scholar: "Ethics, Aesthetics, and the Re-emergence of the Early Bakhtin," led by Caryl Emerson; "Teaching with Bakhtin: Dialogics in Literature, Writing, and Discussion," coordinated by Don Bialostoski; and "Bakhtin, Women Writers, and the Dialogics of Culture," moderated by Laurie Anne Finke. Emerson's workshop became the nexus for the scholarly interactions that would continue over the years and produce the essays in this book. The contributors incorporate a variety of disciplinary backgrounds into their essays, including theatre arts, philosophy, history, women's studies, Latin American literature, and Russian literature. Because of the essays' common origins in the Emerson seminar, their arguments take Bakhtin's ethics and mechanics, as articulated in his writings of 1919 to 1929, and extend them into areas of thought that themselves enter into fruitful dialogue with his theoretical positions. Bakhtin's ideas and vocabulary have become ubiquitous in academic circles and have formed such an intrinsic part of the theoretical underpinnings of many disciplines that, in the spirit of Althusserian interpellation, it is sometimes difficult to determine which set of meanings—Bakhtin's ideas or those of the disciplines themselves—has been constituted by the other. In a scant four decades (a brief period for literary history) Bakhtin studies have come a long way.

The reception of Bakhtin in Russia and the West progressed in different phases: after the excitement surrounding the initial discoveries of his work in Russia in the 1960s, and subsequently in the West in translated editions of the 1980s and early 1990s; after the initial digesting and explicating of his work by scholars in dialogue with each other at conferences and in print; after the widespread appreciation among academics of Bakhtin's work in the richness of its possibilities—after all these journeys of the mind, a new phase of Bakhtin's reception emerged.[1] For Bakhtinians of all persuasions it involves in one of its major strains a *reexamination* of the great thinker's corpus in light of two related concerns: the recovery of Bakhtin as would-be moral and religious philosopher, and investigation of his ethics by means of post-Soviet and postmodernist critical paradigms. Because of his almost limitless applicability to such boundary areas as cultural studies and film studies, among others, Bakhtin has entered the knowledge base and challenged the canonical critical approaches in these areas. In other words, Bakhtin's thought has moved from a state of being studied for itself as object to one of entering and affecting—as a more or less coherent body of theory—the prevailing modes of discourse in the humanities and the social sciences (one can only imagine the headiness of the future incursions of *Bakhtinistika* into the natural sciences). As in the past, this current phase (from the late 1990s to the present time) in the U.S. and Europe emphasized different features of Bakhtin's thought from those that evolved in Russia. Some convergences are becoming manifest, to be sure, but it is safe to say that because of the historical, religious, and cultural differences between the West and Russia, the differences in approach and emphasis between the two groups of Bakhtinists will continue to remain in strong relief with respect to those of the other side.

Typifying this acknowledgment of difference is the question a Russian Bakhtin and Solovyov scholar asked me recently: "Why do American scholars take such unusual approaches to Bakhtin?" His uncomprehending, though well-meaning query belies an academic orientation toward Bakhtin that is embedded in over seventy years of Soviet Russian political culture, religion, and literary theory. While American academic culture was quickly influenced in the mid and late twentieth century by theoretical discoveries in Britain and on the Continent, which culminated in the post-1968 cultural and political reconfigurations (on both sides of the ocean) and attendant embrace of the postmodern mindset, the curriculum of Soviet Russian and post-Soviet academe was evolving by ridding itself of its constricting Marxist framework and reconnecting with its nineteenth- and early-twentieth-century philological past. Although post-Soviet Russia, whether willingly or not, has become a part of the postmodernist world, Bakhtin studies have typically not been situated within this new intellectual and social landscape. As a consequence, among Russian academics Bakhtin is approached respectfully, almost reverently, as one would interact with an Orthodox icon: interest in his work revolves around his contributions to the philosophy of language, moral and ethical philosophy, Dostoevsky's art, and literary theory in general. These critical emphases do not entirely parallel those of the West, whose scholars share Russia's fascination with the aforementioned aspects of Bakhtin's work, but, in addition, have taken their study of his work into such interdisciplinary areas as cultural studies (perhaps the most promising), women's studies, and film studies. For the West, Bakhtin is viewed as more of a literary and cultural theorist, as well as a relativist (whether this is strictly accurate or not) in the postmodern sense, than is the case in Russia.

The book's subtitle, *Ethics and Mechanics*, necessitates some explication. At first glance, the relationship of the two concepts to Bakhtin's thought seems clear to any reader of his work: ethics and mechanics represent, respectively, a body of philosophical ideas and a structural paradigm that may illuminate Bakhtin's ideas for his addressees. The great thinker constructed his complex worldview and expressed his overarching concerns through a highly individualistic moral philosophy. At the same time, however, he remained categorically opposed to both theoretism and determinism. Bakhtin elaborated an ethics that foregrounds morally conceived relationships between individuals in the present time and in unrepeatably evolving (in Bakhtin's sense) circumstances, rather than relationships between the individual and an abstract notion of humanity located somewhere in the future. His ethics is one of the here and now, particularized, and made answerable in the individual human being who has potentially limitless choices to make at every given moment of his or her life. Thus each individual not only accepts full responsibility for his or her thoughts and deeds (the non-alibi in Being), but also possesses unlimited choices, or, to put it another way, a healthy freedom of the will. In all periods of his work Bakhtin rejected any theory that relegated human consciousness and activity to the status of mechanistically determined or teleologically oriented. He considered the unfinalizable, unrepeatable, creating individual too sacred to be reduced to the level of a cog in a machine or Dostoevsky's well-known organ stop. And yet he was influenced by some of the noteworthy developments in science that were appearing in print and being discussed by his close friends and acquaintances: specific questions in biology and the relativity theory in physics interested him and would inform his way of conceptualizing relationships in his ethics and literary theories. [2]

The ethics of Bakhtin's thought constitute the "why" of the process of inquiry: Why is this body of writing on answerability, dialogism, and truth-seeking so vitally important? By comparison, the mechanics of Bakhtin's terminological relationships, and of how his key concepts resonate meaningfully in other texts comprise the "how" of our collection of essays. How can appropriation and recontextualization extend Bakhtin into new aesthetic and ideational realms? The "why" of ethics and "how" of mechanics are similar relationally to that of content and structure in art, but their meanings are recast in order to represent how Bakhtin might have perceived interaction with others, and how scholars today interact both with Bakhtin's thought and with ideas in general. Both are integral to the communication and presentation of ideas, and both fascinated Bakhtin. Even though the word "mechanics" does not figure anywhere in his writings, his intellectual involvement in the scientific thought of his day and commitment to moral relationship building, as evidenced in such concepts as answerability and dialogism, make the term relevant here. Moreover, the process of conveying Bakhtin's ideas in an intertextual and intercultural context underscores the conceptual importance of mechanics, of "the how."

If Bakhtin was concerned with mechanics, however, it was in this sense: although he evolved as a thinker knowledgeable about the major scientific writings and arguments of his day, he abhorred categorical, de-individualizing forms of organization; instead, as Emerson notes, " . . . not unlike the young Wittgenstein, Bakhtin's response was to embrace the *relationalism* dominant for his time while decisively rejecting the *system* that so often and automatically went with it. And why, indeed, must relationships, to be real, arrange themselves into systems?" [emphasis original].[3] When we remind ourselves of Bakhtin's uncompromising view of the individual as a creating, authoring being who can never be repeated, it is easy to understand why and to what degree he would resist a systematization of the experiences that constitute an individual life. Furthermore, in our postmodern world, which foregrounds such characteristics as "the multimedia nature of social life, its polyphony, its heteroglossia, the rapidity of change, the uncritical adoption of modern technology . . . , the absence of historical awareness, [and] the lack of compelling criteria for contextualization, interpretation, and understanding,"[4] Bakhtin's anchoring of his ethical positions in an intended "third consciousness" militates against what Christopher Norris calls "ultra-relativist or [uncritical] consensus-based thinking."[5] Concerning postmodern discourse,

> not only [does it entangle] primary level discourse with secondary or meta-level discourse, but it confounds description with prescription. Insofar as it is description of a state of affairs, we are free to accept or reject it according to its accuracy, its truth value, but insofar as it prescribes . . . a particular orientation toward reality, including perhaps the rejection of those metanarratives that justify our criteria of accuracy and truth, we can neither accept nor reject it according to accuracy and truth.[6]

Thus Bakhtin straddles the fence: his ethics and the metanarratives that inform his theories are firmly rooted in modern, premodern, and Early Christian/Orthodox constructs, while his acceptance of difference and acknowledgment of cultural ambiguity, elevation of character to an almost absolute, independent status (especially with respect to Dostoevsky's heroes), and belief in the individual consciousness (rather than in systems and institutions) fall squarely within the postmodernist ethos.

Since Bakhtin's early philosophical works, such as "Art and Answerability," "Toward a Philosophy of the Act," and "Author and Hero in Aesthetic Activity," are underrepresented in the existing collections of essays associated with Bakhtin, they represent the major fulcrum of our essays' offerings. In their work the essayists endeavor at all times to remain cognizant of both Russian and Western views of

Bakhtin. As a result of the sustained interactions among the book's contributors, as we all realized, not only can any thoughtful encounter with Bakhtin's work be a productive experience, but for the myriad disciplines affected by his work it is no less than transformational. Indeed, Bakhtin's thought exerted a profound, systemic influence on many areas of knowledge as they have been configured in the twentieth century, and the directions taken by recent scholarship promise the same for the twenty-first.[7]

Before turning to the four essays at hand, I consider each concept—ethics and mechanics—separately, in order to clarify further their importance for Bakhtin's thought.

Ethics

The area of philosophical inquiry known as "ethics" makes a number of discrete distinctions, among them one between "objectivism"—"things are good or bad irrespective of personal preferences"—and "subjectivism"—"statements like 'this is good' or 'this ought to be done' are nothing more than expressions of the likes and dislikes of the speaker."[8] Bakhtin's own ethical approach lies somewhere between the two: his ethics involves an individual's reliance on a sensitive network of experiences and decision making in the context of the singular event, but also with some understanding of a moral authority, which is couched in his writings in various ways. Emerson writes of this "third" consciousness, "[a]t different times, Bakhtin writes, this 'invisibly present third party who stands above all the participants in the dialogue' can be God, the Absolute, the dispassionate court of conscience. But for each speaker who shapes an utterance in its direction, this 'third' is always of maximum authority and authorizing power."[9] Bakhtin uses the term "superaddressee" (*nadadresat*) in a related way, to suggest an ideal consciousness against which a speaker frames both spoken and written utterances.[10]

In his work of the 1920s Bakhtin developed a personalist ethics of the unrepeatable and unfinalizable individual who is answerable to other unrepeatable and unfinalizable individuals with whom he or she interacts—Bakhtin's dialogic is conceived in ethical terms and emphasizes that dynamic space between the self and the other. His work evolved in part against the deeply disturbing backdrop of an emergent Bolshevik dictatorship whose Marxist-Leninist ideology reduced the members of society to the status of groups and classes. This reductive mindset made it easier for the Soviet regime to dispense with human lives, for its manipulation of categories and statistics enabled it to avoid being confronted with the suffering of specific individuals. Throughout his life Bakhtin opposed moral and ethical decisions made according to rigid principles and systems, outside of what he terms the "once occurrent" event in "Toward a Philosophy of the Act."

Bakhtin's distinctive and moving ethical thought issues as well from the multi-farious academic subjects in which he steeped himself and in which he was highly proficient. They include the classics, European and Russian literature, the history of philosophy, literary theory, and the philosophy of language. Though his writing manifests a knowledge of Western and Russian religious philosophy (and these subjects are thickly embedded in many of the disciplines he studied and knew well), his personal attitude and intellectual relationship to religion, especially to Orthodox Christianity, remain unclear.[11] No doubt he was familiar with Russian Orthodox theology and liturgical practice, and he may have maintained some association with the Russian Orthodox Church in the 1920s.[12] His philosophy emerges, however, as a secular moral philosophy, containing both neo- and post-Kantian elements, as well as secularized Christian features informed especially by Russian Orthodoxy. Some comments on each of these two influences, philosophical and religious, on Bakhtin's ethics might be useful at this point.

Bakhtin's development as a moral philosopher was enriched by a group of his intellectual friends, who met regularly in the cities of Nivel' and Vitebsk, and later (in a different configuration) in St. Petersburg, to discuss questions primarily, but not exclusively, of German philosophy. Through the influence of Matvei Kagan and other thinkers associated with the neo-Kantians in Marburg, he was able to elaborate the aesthetic concerns most central to his work; among them was the belief that "the two primary aspects of reality were the self and the other, but they did not stand in a dichotomy, for each pole was interrelated with the other."[13] Moreover, Bakhtin, like the neo-Kantians, affirmed that ethics and the "various ways that value [operates] in men's lives" should be the main concern of philosophy.[14] Holquist and Clark note:

> Bakhtin's career may be thought of as part of this ongoing attempt to bring philosophy somehow into congruence with theology. If one were to place him somewhere in a spectrum between the extremes of, let us say, Kant and Pascal, we should have to locate him somewhere closer to Pascal. . . . [However,] [i]n seeking a connection between God and men, Bakhtin concentrated on the forces enabling connections, in society and in language, between men.[15]

Bakhtin's concern about the primacy of ethics for philosophy is refigured in a Christian context, as Mihailovic underscores about "Toward a Philosophy of the Act": "Toward the end of the manuscript [Bakhtin] suggests that his attempt to fully restore ethics to the individual act is tantamount to giving the moral teachings of Christianity a rigorous and finely tuned phenomenological rendering. . . ."[16] In this same work the Christian idea of the incarnation is suggested in Bakhtin's emphasis on the thought's *becoming* ethical only through the act; the source of this emphasis would be Orthodox Christianity, whose theology foregrounds Christ's enfleshment to a much greater degree than does the Western Christian tradition. The thought incarnated as a deed, which includes aesthetic creativity as well as the morally conceived act, can thus be considered ethically redemptive for the individual. An important reason Mihailovic cites for "regarding Bakhtin's relation to theology as being central to his work" is as follows: " . . . [it is] the sheer density, paradigmatic clarity, and deliberate orchestration of Bakhtin's theologically inspired terms and conceptual categories. . . . Theological categories and terms recalling christology in general and Trinitarianism in particular emerge in almost every essay in Bakhtin's long and varied career."[17] Although Bakhtin utilized these categories and concepts structurally, rather than philosophically, their centrality and metaphoric consistency in his writing point to a significance for the whole of his thought that goes beyond solely a structural one. Thus the mechanics—or concept and category building—become integral to Bakhtin's ethics.

Bakhtin's stances vis-à-vis ethics raise two intriguing questions that are relevant for our present task. The first concerns whether an ethics can exist outside of religion. Fyodor Dostoevsky and Vladimir Solovyov, for example, maintained that it could not, and in this regard their position is aligned with the West's and Russia's metaphysical tradition.[18] Empiricism, however, which emphasizes that we gain knowledge about the world through our sense experiences, would validate the opposite: that it is entirely possible for an ethics to exist outside of any religious framework, taking as its source of legitimacy, at least in part, the idea that a code of laws can be mutually agreed upon and followed by the members of any civil society. Bertrand Russell, considered by many the "father" of logical positivism, presents a case in point of this latter approach: he could not reconcile to himself the idea of a loving and powerful God with the existence of so much suffering in the world, and maintained the position that religion through the ages has done considerable harm to humanity.[19] Bakhtin as both a thinker in the Christian tradition and a philosopher may have reconciled the two views, metaphysical and empiricist, in such a way that he used Christian ideas and scientific discoveries paradigmatically, still locating moral authority outside the individual along the lines of Christian theology, yet secularizing the relationship between the self and the other (the latter construed variously as "God," a "third," or "superaddressee") in his work.

A second question regarding ethics and Bakhtin suggests itself as well, and concerns the existence of the concept of truth. The question can be broken down into two corollaries of each other. Can truth exist outside of language? Can truth exist outside of religion? Some philosophers of language, such as Russell and Rudolf Carnap, posit that truth is a property of language, and that the smallest

linguistic unit in which it manifests itself is the sentence, since a completed, organized thought (a proposition) is possible only at that semantic level. Moreover,
philosophies of language typically distinguish, as Bakhtin does in his ethics, between private and public expressions of language. Private language involves what
we think when we are alone with our thoughts, while public language encompasses
not only verbal statements but public acts as well, the "going out once and for all"
from within the self. An individual's ethics, his or her personal truth, would be
made manifest in such public language (as a form of this individual's participation
in Being). Ethical truth for Bakhtin is actualized by such public expressions of language, in a language that is appropriately referential—the community of speakers
of which the individual is a part understands and accepts the meanings and values
inherent in the words chosen by that individual. Bakhtin's ethics depend heavily
on specific circumstances, although not entirely so, since we know that he did
not accept pure relativism. We are again reminded that a "third" consciousness,
or "superaddressee," comes into play at an important point of the truth-defining
process during a particular event.

In this vein, in his *Problems of Dostoevsky's Poetics* Bakhtin elevates the image of
Christ as truth-bearing, but not necessarily dogmatic. His description of Dostoevsky's conception of Christ offers Christ as the supreme ethical source:

> . . . the image of Christ represents for him [Dostoevsky] the resolution of
> ideological quests. This image or this highest voice must crown the world
> of voices, must organize and subdue it. . . . A quest for truth not as the de-
> duction of one's own consciousness, in fact not in the monologic context of
> an individual consciousness at all, but rather in the ideal authoritative image
> of another human being, an orientation toward the other's voice, the other's
> word: all this is characteristic of Dostoevsky's form-shaping ideology.[20]

When we take Bakhtin's statement about Dostoevsky's art in the context
of his own writing of the 1920s, with his concern for dialogue and community
life as ethical processes, it is not difficult to conclude that Christ represented
for him as well "the ideal authoritative image of another human being," but one
oriented "toward the other's voice, toward the other's word." Bakhtin's ethics thus
can accommodate degrees of truthfulness and resists such a thing as absolute
truth. Emerson interprets the relationship implied here as follows: "Genuine truth
always involves more work and more risk than dogma or propositions require of us.
Because the task of life is always posited and created rather than merely given, any
truth we might achieve in life is available only as a relationship."[21] What stands
out in Bakhtin's thought is the dynamic state of *truth seeking* by means of certain
moral compasses, not the potentially dangerous illusion of a complete attainment
of truth.

Mechanics

While the present book's connection with Bakhtin's ethical philosophy is unambiguous, its engagement with mechanics may not be as readily apparent. The word "mechanics" immediately calls to mind the process by which something works, which includes some sort of agent or catalyst that causes the process to go forward. "Process" in turn suggests movement, a phenomenon that is dynamic and evolving, rather than static and completed or fully formed. The discussion below considers three interrelated connotations of "mechanics" that are relevant to this book's essays. They are (1) in a general sense, the mechanics of how things work, of how particular elements of a whole become cornerstones without which the whole cannot function, (2) the mechanics of empiricism and positivism in the area of philosophy of science (which informed Bakhtin's thought during the 1920s), and (3) the intellectual, "organic" mechanics of conceptual relationships, of considering concepts in their original usage and reframing them in a new text, producing ideally a state of cross-fertilization for both the concepts and their new contexts. All three connotations of mechanics may comprise a scaffolding of intellectual pathways that contributed to the development of Bakhtin's ethical ideas, as well as the application of them by the authors below to new aesthetic subjects.

To be sure, while Bakhtin remained deeply suspicious of categories in his ethics, he nevertheless was intrigued by the systems and processes of scientific discoveries. He wanted to study and understand how things work, in order to ground his own conceptual and theoretical work in well-established patterns of inquiry in the sciences as well as the humanities.[22] Concerning empiricism and positivism, a negative and then a positive definition (both in light of Bakhtin's thought) related to the concept of mechanics may be useful here. In the first, "mechanism" may be described as the "[t]heory that all phenomena are totally explicable on mechanical principles. . . . In general the view that nature consists merely of material in motion, and that it operates automatically."[23] The second characterizes "mechanics" as "[t]he science of motion, affording theoretical description by means of specification of position of particles bound by relations to other particles. . . . This involves space and time and frames of reference (in a relative fashion)."[24] The two cited definitions seem to capture both aspects of empiricist-positivist mechanics that are germane to Bakhtin's ethics of the 1920s. The first encapsulates everything that was abhorrent to Bakhtin about deterministic conceptualizations of life and history, namely that "all phenomena" can be completely explained ("finalized," as he would put it) according to "mechanical principles." Bakhtin affirmed instead a philosophy that not only elevated individual choice and responsibility, but also lent dignity to the creative and unpredictable ("noncoincidental") aspects of an individual's life experiences.

The second, more positive definition of "mechanics" seems uncannily ap-
plicable to Bakhtin's thought if we change the scientific context to a humanistic one, and especially if we substitute the words "human being" or "literary
character" for "particle." The result comes close to characterizing Bakhtin's openended (though not relativist or chaotic), yet morally responsible philosophy of
human relationships.[25] To elaborate: the notion of "particles bound by relations
to other particles . . . [involving] space and time and frames of reference" evokes
Bakhtin's ethics of individuals bound by their everyday ("prosaic," as Gary Saul
Morson and Caryl Emerson would describe it)[26] relations to other individuals,
which involve space and time and varying circumstances. The definition implies
a mechanics, not of categories and sets, but rather as a process and an ongoing
event, concepts much more congenial for Bakhtin's thought. It does not seem too
far an intellectual stretch to draw parallels, albeit in a limited way, between the
interrelationships among particles and those among individuals, especially since
we know that Bakhtin paid particular attention to evolving thought in the sciences,
to models and relationships he noted in those disciplines that he felt would help
him to clarify aspects of his own theoretical work in the humanities. Comparisons such as the stated one between particles and individuals are not unusual,
and philosophers often utilize them to advance their arguments. For example,
Vladimir Solovyov (whose work Bakhtin knew) begins his *Philosophical Principles
of Integral Knowledge* (Filosofskie nachala tsel'nogo znaniia, 1877) with an extended
and elaborate description of the interconnected parts of a biological organism as
analogous to the relationship throughout history of the individual to political,
economic, and spiritual societies. The aforementioned references to "space and
time and frames of reference" are reminiscent of Bakhtin's complex idea of the
"chronotope,"[27] one largely dependent on spatial and temporal indicators. Clark
and Holquist note in this context:

> Bakhtin, in arguing that the particular place from which something is per-
> ceived determines the meaning of what is observed, was attempting to do
> for the conscious mind what Einstein was seeking to do for the physical
> universe when he, too, at almost the same time, emphasized the determining
> role played by the locus from which phenomena are observed.[28]

> Bakhtin looked to the sciences, among other disciplines, for paradigms of
> and insights into human relationships, which he could then work out in his
> own terms in a different area of inquiry.[29]

The third connotation of "mechanics"—as an intellectual, "organic," fruc-
tifying process that occurs between texts—may be clarified vis-à-vis Bakhtin if
we recall Solovyov's discussion in his *Lectures on Divine Humanity* (Chteniia o bogoche-

lovechestve, 1878–81) of "organic thinking" as a more integral approach to the study of ideas. Solovyov writes, *"organic thinking* considers an object in its all-sided whole-nesss and, consequently, in its inner bond with all the other objects . . . organic thinking can be called a developing or evolving type of thinking . . ."* (emphasis original).[30] This type of thinking is essentially the same as Bakhtin's "participa-tive thinking" *(uchastnoe myshlenie)* in "Toward a Philosophy of the Act": Bakhtin describes those who seek to resolve the relationship between theoretical and actual Being as "those who know how not to detach their performed act from its product, but rather how to relate both of them to the unitary and unique context of life and seek to determine them in that context as an indivisible unity."[31]

Is it ultimately profitable for us in a study of Bakhtin to consider such links between science and literary theory, or between science and moral philosophy? An answer may be a cautious "yes," if we bear in mind that the second, more positive definition of mechanics (in its connection with empiricism and positivism) describes what the contributors to this collection of essays (individually and taken together) hope to accomplish: to work toward an epistemology of Bakhtin's early thought by (1) discussing some of the essential features of his philosophy of human relationships, and (2) establishing meaningful connections between these features and relevant disciplinary work as it is evolving today. The establishment of connections in turn constitutes a mechanics of intertextuality: between science and literary theory, science and moral philosophy, and Bakhtin's theories and literature. Thus, for both Bakhtin and the authors of these essays the activity of "participative thinking" (a kind of "organic" mechanics) involves the ethically driven process of truth seeking, concept and category building, and intertextual as well as intercultural communication.

Broadly speaking, from the perspective of intellectual history, we can allow ourselves to develop the above connections, because Bakhtin himself ranged so far and wide in his inquiries into various fields of knowledge. In this regard, an accurate representation of the scope of the issues spotlighted by our collec-tion's authors would have to involve both ethics and mechanics: the authors are concerned with Bakhtin's ethics, to be sure, but they also investigate *relationships* within Bakhtin's body of thought and analyze the *methods* and *processes* by which creative individuals interact with their artistic offspring and seek to explain various phenomena in the world. In this way, mechanics for the writers of these essays become a methodology for making carefully considered theoretical claims and underscoring Bakhtin's deeply humanistic emphasis in his works. In their work the essayists kept the premise in mind that Bakhtin's more global concepts can operate in other texts without distorting their original meanings. Hence the application of Bakhtin's terms to the problematics of specific literary works becomes a process of intellectual and "organic" mechanics, with the hoped-for result being a rich engagement of Bakhtin's concepts with a new field of meanings.

The Essays Themselves

Let me now offer a few words about the individual essays in the collection. My comments are intended to situate the ideas in the essays within the ethics/mechanics framework, and reflect on the growing significance of Bakhtin's early works for postmodern paradigms of the individual and culture, as configured in various disciplines. Bakhtin's ethics represent a subject much written about and typically included in analyses of his diverse corpus, but in the present collection the authors attempt to widen the lens and sharpen the focus, in the hopes of positioning Bakhtin in a more illuminating way with respect to the "why" and the "how" of his spectrum of thought.[32] The authors explore various ethical relationships, offering examples from drama, literature, theology, cultural politics, and nationalist theory.

As noted earlier, the four essays under consideration concern themselves with Bakhtin's ethics, and their arguments are buttressed either formally by his writings of the 1920s or in a general way by some of the key concepts Bakhtin first articulated during that decade, with plans to develop them further at some later point. One such concept is "dialogism," which in Bakhtin's philosophical Weltanschauung is linked organically with the search for truth, the rejection of a finalized notion of truth or teleological approach to human existence, and the humble, yet ennobling acknowledgment that each individual participates in a unique way in this ongoing process of self-discovery. Moreover, dialogism contains within itself the important idea of community (Christianity's concept of "brotherhood," conceptualized in Russian Orthodoxy as *sobornost'* or "communitarianism"), which Bakhtin understood in ethical terms, in the relationship between the self and the other: the individual in his or her daily life does not exist in a vacuum, but interacts with others socially in a presumably meaningful framework and linguistically within the levels and gradations of verbal expression Bakhtin termed "heteroglossia." Hence he or she is answerable in an absolute sense to those others. Bakhtin's conception of community appears to be informed by Orthodox Christian doctrine concerning the created world, the transfiguration of the body, and redemption, as Timothy Ware [Bishop Kallistos] explains:

> . . . deification is not a solitary but a "social process" . . . as the three persons of the Godhead "dwell" in one another, so we must "dwell" in our fellow humans, living not for ourselves alone, but in and for others. . . . love of God and of our fellow humans must be practical: Orthodoxy rejects all forms of Quietism, all types of love which do not issue in action. Deification, while it includes the heights of mystical experience, has also a very prosaic and down-to-earth aspect.[33]

Each of the four essays interacts with the concept of "dialogism": the first investigates dialogue qua search for truth, as aesthetic, dramatic truth, while the remaining three ponder the literary act as an extension of personal, experiential truth. The last three essays in particular are concerned with questions of the "act" and of "answerability," as Bakhtin understood these terms. All of the essays engage the idea of authority in different ways that are relevant for Bakhtin's thought. The first, David Krasner's "Dialogics and Dialectics: Bakhtin, Young Hegelians, and Dramatic Theory," explores two diametrically opposed dramatic theories—Hegel's dialectics (with the Young Hegelian revision of them) and Bakhtin's dialogics. To accomplish this, Krasner divides his argument into five sections: four on theory and the last on two proof plays. In the theoretical sections he provides, first, an overview of Hegelian dialectics and their application to drama, followed by the reception of dialectics by the Young Hegelians in the 1840s (with their rejection of Hegel's ideas of synthesis and reconciliation), and, finally, an examination of Bakhtin's dialogism in the context of both Hegelian and Young Hegelian monologism. Appreciative of both theoretical approaches and their aesthetic possibilities, Krasner aims to "show that [Bakhtin's] dialogism is of value to dramatic theory," despite the fact that Bakhtin's own emphasis in his theory and criticism of literature lies elsewhere, on the novel.

After providing a historical overview of both philosophical systems, Krasner applies dialectics and dialogics, respectively, to plays he considers representative of each theoretical approach: August Wilson's *The Piano Lesson* (1987) and Ntozake Shange's *for colored girls who have considered suicide/when the rainbow is enuf* (1976). His application of the dialectic and dialogic theories to specific examples of the dramatic repertoire turns on the ethical implications in drama (both for the characters within and the audience/readers without) of a fictional world containing an ultimate resolution for two conflicting, yet equally persuasive, morally driven points of view, as contrasted with a created world in which all of the characters' voices and that of the author are of equal validity and require each other's presence for their affirmation. Krasner notes in conclusion that the distinction between dialectics and dialogics lies not so much in their relationship to synthesis, but rather in how they interpret difference. The Hegelians and Young Hegelians elevate the struggle of competing voices as essential to dramatic action, whereas Bakhtin's dialogics enable the fruitful existence of a multiplicity of voices and views, but without the merging or disappearance of any participating entity. For Bakhtin, it is the process of becoming—not the drive toward and achievement of wholeness—that represents dramatic and real-life truth.

The question of authority enters into the arguments offered by the authors of the remaining three essays, and functions in a variety of relationships, both abstract and personal: between two fictional characters, between author and hero, between individual and idea, between interviewer and interviewee, between author and homeland. In the second essay, "Bakhtin's Ethics and an Iconographic Standard in *Crime and Punishment*" by Jacqueline Zubeck, the author reads Raskolnikov's ethical dilemma in *Crime and Punishment* in light of Bakhtin's "Art and Answerability" and

"Toward a Philosophy of the Act." Her analysis of Raskolnikov's moral dilemma reveals how Dostoevsky's character personifies Bakhtin's worst fears concerning theoretism by playing out in his mind the "disembodied consciousness" that tries to ignore its own unique, answerable place in the world. Raskolnikov's authority remains "a set of utilitarian principles which are consistent within a narrow rationalist framework." The essay's real tour de force, however, lies in its illuminating analysis of Raskolnikov as an iconographic image, one that takes into itself the richness and theological complexity of the Eastern Orthodox pictorial tradition. Zubeck links Bakhtin and Dostoevsky to what she calls an "iconographic standard," "a perspective which is connected thematically, technically, narratively, and visually to the icon." These connections are convincing precisely because of the complex of meanings—aesthetic, religious, historical, and ethical—that are embedded in the icon and iconography, meanings that imply and encourage a personal relationship with a higher consciousness. Such an ethically charged relationship was central to Bakhtin's theories of the "act" and dialogue, according to which any communicative act posits the existence of an ideal, interested listener.

The third and fourth essays engage authority in the realm of power structures between individuals in a changing cultural and political environment, exploring the process—the mechanics—by which the relationships among writer, text, and reader can become politicized. Kimberly Nance offers the third essay, "Let Us Say That There Is a Human Being before Me Who Is Suffering: Empathy, Exotopy, and Ethics in the Reception of Latin American Collaborative *Testimonio*," in which Bakhtin's ethical writings interact powerfully with the concept and practice of *testimonio*. The author defines *testimonio* as a Latin American genre in which "a speaking subject narrates her experience of political violence as part of a project of ameliorating social injustice." Drawing upon recent events involving individuals in Latin American literature and culture, Nance examines the stages of *testimonio* (finding a voice, taking part in the act of communication, and weighing the potential effects of the spoken and written word on various actors in the process), and reflects upon its problematics and significance in literary, cultural, and sociopolitical contexts. Her excellent use of interview material in the essay reveals the psychology underlying the relationship between a persecuted, disenfranchised woman and a privileged professional writer for what it is: an interaction in which the interlocutors are not equal and in which the potential for subtle, even unwitting manipulation on both sides is omnipresent.

Nance makes two important points: (1) that a marked divergence in perspectives on and assessment of the purpose of *testimonio* exists between the "speaking subjects" and the writers/critics, and (2) that the question of answerability linked with the *testimonio* remains a complex one that no one should expect to see fully resolved in the near future. She manifests an intelligent sympathy for both sides in the relationship, concluding that *testimonio's* potential has not been exhausted and depends on the respect (through the Bakhtinian ethical processes of empathy and exotopy) both sides must give to each other and to their intended reading audience. Despite the difficulties both sides of such a collaboration encounter in transforming politically caused suffering into the possibility for social justice, all does not seem lost, as Bakhtin's last documented written words remind us: "nothing is absolutely dead; every meaning will someday have its homecoming festival."[34] Indeed, during seventy years of Soviet oppression, the printed word provided inspiration and a voice for those who otherwise had no avenue for the expression of their suffering.

The conviction that all is not lost is underscored similarly in the fourth contribution, my own: I examine literature by the Russian Village Prose writers Viktor Astafiev, Valentin Rasputin, and Vladimir Soloukhin as literature of answerability (in Bakhtin's special understanding of the term) in which Russia emerges as a chronotope. My essay involves the process by which these writers conceptualize Russia in works that combine aesthetic with patriotic (and, indirectly, political) considerations, but which present Russia as following a long established pattern of signification. For the three authors, authority resides in their personal experiences and literary interpretation of seventy years of Soviet rule and their resulting ethical act of committing their thoughts to paper: the "going out once and for all" from within the self. I attempt to situate the image of Russia both within Bakhtin's early philosophical works and within the extensive body of writing termed the "Russian idea" (much of which was known to Bakhtin). The product of this writing—a complex image of Russia that continues to resonate in contemporary Russian belles lettres—might prompt a reexamination of how Russia is figured in nineteenth- and twentieth-century Russian literature.

The four essays implicitly explore various features of the mechanics issue: How can Bakhtin's key theoretical concepts be productively appropriated and applied to literary and nonliterary texts? How can these concepts provide structural as well as thematic underpinnings to the works? Of paramount concern to the essayists is mechanics as an intellectual latticework spanning decades and cultures that connects Bakhtin's original thought to the truth-seeking process they examine in the respective texts. Keeping both normative and empirical considerations in mind, the essayists assemble and analyze various types of knowledge and information connected with Bakhtin's writing in order to reveal why Bakhtin in particular offers a productive avenue of interpretation for the relevant texts.

Each of these essays interacts in its own way with Bakhtin's eloquently elaborated belief that individual answerability lies in a thought's entering the world (Being) and being translated, transformed into a specific action (the act). The contributors thus demonstrate the broad applicability of Bakhtin's ethical paradigms and literary constructs to a variety of contexts, both theoretical and practical, through the centuries and in modern times. In the face of increasing public skepticism and criticism of academe, which are embedded in the postmodern challenge to any established forms of authority, intellectual or otherwise, the authors of these essays affirm "that theory has 'consequences' beyond the professional or academic sphere, and that the question whether or not to 'do theory' is always within reach of the larger question whether *anything* we do or think is likely to affect the course of social or political events" [emphasis original].[35] It is surely the case, however, that some theories, some cornerstones of thought, are more vibrant and enduring than others; one senses that we have only scratched the surface of what Bakhtin's thought can offer us.

May the dialogue and the search for truth, in the spirit of Bakhtinian unfinalizability, both continue. . . .

Notes

My gratitude goes to my husband, Richard Nollan, for sharing with me many of his insights into philosophy and the history and philosophy of science. I also am indebted to Caryl Emerson, Gary Saul Morson, and the anonymous readers for their helpful suggestions concerning this introduction.

1. For a more comprehensive presentation of Bakhtin's reception in Russia and the West, see Caryl Emerson, Introduction, in *Critical Essays on Mikhail Bakhtin*, ed. Emerson (New York: G. K. Hall and Co., 1999), 1–26.

2. See Katerina Clark and Michael Holquist, *Mikhail Bakhtin* (Cambridge, Mass.: Harvard University Press, 1984), 66 ff., for an account of Bakhtin's interest in biology and its connection with the self/other relationship, which provides for Bakhtin one of the foundations of understanding the self and of identity formation. See also 102 for a description of Bakhtin's acquaintance with I. I. Kanaev, who "was instrumental in interesting Bakhtin in questions of biology, especially those concerning the relationship of mind to matter and body to spirit." In her introductory comments to a recent collection of essays on Bakhtin, Emerson points out, "[w]e must remember that Bakhtin . . . began his career in an era obsessed with mathematical essences, functions, and formal categories such as sets, fields, groups" (23). See Emerson, Introduction, in *Bakhtin in Contexts: Across the Disciplines*, ed. Amy Mandelker (Evanston, Ill.: Northwestern University Press, 1995), 1–30.

3. Emerson, Introduction, *Bakhtin in Contexts: Across the Disciplines*, 23.

4. See Vincent Crapanzano, "The Postmodern Crisis: Discourse, Parody, Memory," in Mandelker, ed. *Bakhtin in Contexts: Across the Disciplines*, 137–50, esp. 140.

5. Christopher Norris, *What's Wrong With Postmodernism: Critical Theory and the Ends of Philosophy* (Baltimore: Johns Hopkins University Press, 1990), 6. Norris

continues on the same page, "And it is all the more important to sustain [arguments opposed to the postmodernist pragmatist view] at a time when 'public opinion' in the West is subject to a vast range of manipulative pressures—always in the name of freedom, democracy, rational self-interest, etc.—whose effect is precisely to reinforce such uncritical consensus values."

6. Crapanzano, 141.

7. For a fascinating overview of Bakhtin in the twentieth century, see Emerson, *The First Hundred Years of Mikhail Bakhtin* (Princeton: Princeton University Press, 1997), esp. 4–122.

8. W. F. Bynum, E. J. Browne, and Roy Porter, eds., *Dictionary of the History of Science* (Princeton: Princeton University Press, 1981), 405.

9. Emerson, Introduction, *Bakhtin in Contexts: Across the Disciplines*, 21.

10. See Emerson, Introduction, 20–22; and Gary Saul Morson, "Prosaic Bakhtin: *Landmarks*, Anti-Intelligentsialism, and the Russian Countertradition," 34 (both essays appear in *Bakhtin in Contexts: Across the Disciplines*).

11. See Alexandar Mihailovic, *Corporeal Words: Mikhail Bakhtin's Theology of Discourse* (Evanston, Ill.: Northwestern University Press, 1997); and Emerson, "Russian Orthodoxy and the Early Bakhtin," *Religion and Literature* 22, 2–3 (summer–autumn 1990), 109–31. Vadim Kozhinov noted in an interview, "I remember asking [Bakhtin] once how one was to respond to the different directions of Christianity. He answered me . . . that a human being born in Russia could not help but be Orthodox, that it was an absolute necessity. . . . At the same time . . . his religious convictions were noncanonical, which is typical of all Russian religious thinkers of the twentieth century." See Nicholas Rzhevsky, "Kozhinov on Bakhtin," in Emerson, ed., *Critical Essays on Mikhail Bakhtin*, 52–66, esp. 57–59.

12. See Clark and Holquist, *Mikhail Bakhtin*, esp. 120–45; and Emerson, "Russian Orthodoxy and the Early Bakhtin," 109–13. Clark and Holquist consider Bakhtin to have remained a "believer in the Orthodox tradition all his life" (120) and locate his thought squarely within the Russian religio-philosophical tradition. Emerson generally concurs with their estimation of the role Russian Orthodox theology played in Bakhtin's philosophical writing, but points out as well Vadim Liapunov's assessment that Bakhtin may instead have been "contributing to a perfectly conventional German academic tradition, *Religionsphilosophie*" (110). She situates Bakhtin's work vis-à-vis religion between these two convincing positions, concluding that "Bakhtin can be said to qualify as a thinker in the Russian Orthodox tradition" (113). Emerson notes that "Mihailovic properly numbers among Bakhtin's inspirations both the fourth-century Church father John Chrysostom and the nineteenth-century philosopher critic Vladimir Soloviev" in his "Bakhtin and the Growth of Russian Theology" (127, note 13). Soloviev's lifelong attempts to elaborate a synthetic religious philosophy that was all-inclusive no doubt would have appealed to Bakhtin, as would Chrysostom's spiritual and aesthetic achieve-

ments as editor of one of the two major liturgies of the Orthodox Christian Church. Moreover, Chrysostom's compassion toward the people he served, his humility, and also his "non-coincidence" (with himself) would have attracted Bakhtin as well: Chrysostom's unexpected self-effacement and elevation of his close friend Basil (the Great) at the time of their proposed ordination as priests presents a case in point. See [Saint] John Chrysostom, *On the Priesthood: A Treatise in Six Books*, tr. [Rev.] Patrick Boyle (Westminster, Md.: The Newman Bookshop, 1945), esp. Books I and II.

13. James M. [Michael] Holquist and Katerina Clark, "The Influence of Kant in the Early Work of M. M. Bakhtin," in *Literary Theory and Criticism: Festschrift Presented to René Wellek in Honor of His Eightieth Birthday*, vol. 1 (Bern, New York: Peter Lang, 1984), 304. Holquist and Clark's article provides a fuller discussion of the influence of Kant and the neo-Kantians on Bakhtin's intellectual development than is possible in this introduction. See also Clark and Holquist, *Mikhail Bakhtin*, 35–119.

14. Ibid., 306.

15. Ibid., 309.

16. Mihailovic, 56–57.

17. Ibid., 4–5.

18. See S. M. Solov'ev, *Vladimir Solov'ev: Zhizn' i tvorcheskaia èvoliutsiia* (Moscow: Respublika, 1997), 310–11 ff. In a letter written in 1884, Solov'ev states: "I don't separate ethics from religion . . ." [translation mine]; in later years the connection he elaborated between those two subjects became less direct, though it was retained.

19. See Bertrand Russell, *Why I Am Not a Christian*, ed. Paul Edwards (New York: Simon and Schuster, 1967), esp. 3–47.

20. Mikhail Bakhtin, "The Idea in Dostoevsky," in *Problems of Dostoevsky's Poetics*, ed. and tr. Caryl Emerson, Theory and History of Literature, Vol. 8 (Minneapolis: University of Minnesota Press, 1984), 97–98. The quoted lines, in Emerson's translation, are exactly the same in both the original book (M. M. Bakhtin, *Problemy tvorchestva Dostoevskogo* [Leningrad: Priboi, 1929], 89–90) and the 1963 redaction. The value of the image of Christ for Bakhtin's thought is also noted by Emerson, "Russian Orthodoxy and the Early Bakhtin," 113.

21. Emerson, "Russian Orthodoxy and the Early Bakhtin," 113.

22. In this context it is useful to recall that in Russia (which followed the European philological tradition) literature and the other humanities are considered "sciences," and therefore the gap for Bakhtin between the two intellectual pursuits remained much narrower than is the case in the American educational system.

23. Dagobert D. Runes, ed., *Dictionary of Philosophy* (Totowa, N.J.: Littlefield, Adams and Co., 1972), 194.

24. Ibid.

25. For an explication of the problematics of Bakhtin's poetics (both in his

work and in its interpretation), see Emerson, "Problems with Baxtin's Poetics," *Slavic and East European Journal* 32, no. 4 (winter 1988), 503–25. Among other key concepts, Emerson discusses relativism, closure, openness, outside perspective, the embodied other, and the connection between aesthetics and ethics in Bakhtin's works and worldview.

26. See Morson and Emerson, *Mikhail Bakhtin: Creation of a Prosaics* (Stanford, Calif.: Stanford University Press, 1990), esp. Part I, Chapter 1, 15–62.

27. See M. M. Bakhtin, "Forms of Time and Chronotope in the Novel," in *The Dialogic Imagination: Four Essays by M. M. Bakhtin*, ed. Michael Holquist, tr. Emerson and Michael Holquist (Austin: University of Texas Press, 1981), 84–258. Several quotes from this essay are noteworthy. The first, which reminds us of the scientific origin of Bakhtin's concept of "space-time" (crucial for his "chronotope"), is as follows:

> We will give the name *chronotope* (literally, "time space") to the intrinsic connectedness of temporal and spatial relationships that are artistically expressed in literature. This term [space-time] is employed in mathematics, and was introduced as part of Einstein's Theory of Relativity. The special meaning it has in relativity theory is not important for our purposes; we are borrowing it for literary criticism almost as a metaphor (almost, but not entirely). (84)

In the second, the scientific language evolves into an artistic humanism reminiscent of Christian "enfleshment":

> In the literary artistic chronotope, spatial and temporal indicators are fused into one carefully thought-out, concrete whole. Time, as it were, thickens, takes on flesh, becomes artistically visible; likewise, space becomes charged and responsive to the movements of time, plot, and history. This intersection of axes and fusion of indicators characterizes the artistic chronotope. . . . The chronotope as a formally constitutive category determines to a significant degree the image of man in literature as well. The image of man is always intrinsically chronotopic. (84–85)

28. Clark and Holquist, 69.

29. In this context Albert Einstein's letter to a sixth grade child who had asked him whether scientists pray and what they pray for is revealing:

> Scientific research is based on the idea that everything that takes place is determined by laws of nature, and therefore this holds for the actions of people. For this reason, a research scientist will hardly be inclined to believe

that events could be influenced by prayer, i.e., by a wish addressed to a supernatural Being.

However, it must be admitted that our actual knowledge of these laws is only imperfect and fragmentary, so that, actually, the belief in the existence of basic all-embracing laws in Nature also rests on a sort of faith. All the same this faith has been largely justified so far by the success of scientific research.

But, on the other hand, every one who is seriously involved in the pursuit of science becomes convinced that a spirit is manifest in the laws of the Universe—a spirit vastly superior to that of man, and one in the face of which we with our modest powers must feel humble.

See *Albert Einstein: The Human Side*, ed. Helen Dukas and Banesh Hoffmann (Princeton, N.J.: Princeton University Press, 1979), 27–29.

30. Vladimir Solovyov, *Lectures on Divine Humanity*, revised and ed. Boris Jakim tr. Peter Zouboff (Hudson, N.Y.: Lindisfarne Press, 1995), 89–90. To be sure, Solovyov's argument opposes "mechanical thinking," which "takes objects in their abstract separateness . . . ," with "organic thinking," which "considers an object in its all-sided wholeness. . . ." Solovyov further describes "mechanical (rationalist) thinking" as "only a contrasting and combining type of thinking," whereas "organic thinking" is "a developing or evolving type of thinking" (90). The mechanics envisioned in this collection conflates both types of thinking in their most hopeful connotations (in an attempt as well to be faithful to Bakhtin's intentions), but especially as typical and necessary for human inquiry into the relationships between various subjects.

31. M. M. Bakhtin, *Toward a Philosophy of the Act*, trans. Vadim Liapunov, ed. Michael Holquist and Vadim Liapunov (Austin: University of Texas Press, 1993), 19 (Bakhtin's footnote). See also 86, note 29.

32. A great deal of investigative work remains for Bakhtin scholars concerned with his ethics and "organic" mechanics, particularly in the areas of his religio-philosophical views (which form a crucial component of his work of the 1920s) and his intellectual links with the sciences (especially biology and physics) and the philosophy of science.

33. Timothy Ware [Bishop Kallistos], *The Orthodox Church* (New York: Penguin, 1993), 237.

34. M. M. Bakhtin, "K metodologii gumanitarnykh nauk," *Èstetika slovesnogo tvorchestva* (Moscow: Iskusstvo, 1979), 373. Translated by and quoted in Clark and Holquist, 350. Bakhtin's infinite faith in the power of the future to recover all possible meanings of the word and the act seems strikingly similar to Nikolai Fedorov's conception of recovering the entire external world in a universal resurrection, in the latter's *The Philosophy of the Common Task* (1906, 1913). Fedorov

writes: "we deem it possible . . . to achieve through all the people . . . knowledge and control of all the molecules and atoms of the external world in such a way as to collect the dispersed, to unite the decomposed . . . into bodies which they had at their death. . . ." (*Philosophy of the Common Task,* vol. 1, 289, 330–31, 442). Translated by and quoted in Ludmila Koehler, *N. F. Fedorov: The Philosophy of Action* (Pittsburgh, Pa.: Institute for the Human Sciences, 1979). The similarity between Bakhtin's and Fedorov's ideas on "human immortality" is noted in passing in Clark and Holquist, 314. To be sure, this is a foundational Christian concept as well ("Are not five sparrows sold for two farthings, and not one of them is forgotten before God? But even the very hairs of your head are all numbered. Fear not therefore: ye are of more value than many sparrows" [Luke 12: 6–7, King James translation]). Moreover, the Orthodox Christian liturgy (which is celebrated at least once per week) contains the phrase "always, now, and forever," indicating a timelessness and permanence to God's knowledge of all things in all their meanings.

35. Norris, 5.

Bakhtin

Dialogics and Dialectics: Bakhtin, Young Hegelians, and Dramatic Theory

David Krasner

Introduction: Dialogics and Dramatic Theory

With the noteworthy exception of articles by Marvin Carlson and Helene Keyssar,[1] few have attempted to establish a comparison between Bakhtin's thought and dramatic theory. The reason may seem obvious: there is nothing in the literary criticism of Bakhtin's corpus which would encourage drama as dialogic. Bakhtin's stock is in the novel, particularly Dostoevsky's novels, as a literary genre that he considers the greatest source of dialogism.[2] In his *Problems of Dostoevsky's Poetics*, Bakhtin states that drama is "encased in a firm and stable monologic framework." He adds further that drama fails to relinquish the monologic form because "rejoinders in a dramatic dialogue do not rip apart the represented world, do not make it multi-leveled; on the contrary, if they are authentically dramatic, these rejoinders necessitate the utmost monolithic unity of that world. In drama the world must be made from a single piece." For Bakhtin, any "weakening of this monolithic quality leads to a weakening of dramatic effect. The characters come together dialogically in the unified field of vision of author, director, and audience, against the clearly defined background of a single-tiered world."[3]

Bakhtin excludes drama from the field of dialogism because, as we have just seen, for him drama does not allow for the weakening of the monologic effect, nor does it allow for an "all-encompassing language, dialogically oriented to separate languages."[4] Bakhtin, however, does not consider the fact that drama presents live actors on stage, physically voicing utterances without an author's presence. Although the words are the author's, the voices are not. The presence of different people does "rip apart the represented world," separated by different beings in constant, interactive dialogue. Moreover, dialogue, as Helene Keyssar argues, "*is* the action in theatre, and any action on stage is refracted (to use another Bakhtinian term) through the diverse points of view of writers, actors, designers, and spectators."[5] Drama demands, as Bakhtin says of the novel, a "dialogic communion *between*

3

consciousnesses." The "idea" presented in literature, Bakhtin asserts, "is a live *event*, played out at the point of dialogic meeting between two or several conscious-nesses. In this sense the idea is similar to the word, with which it is dialogically united. Like the word, the idea wants to be heard, understood, and 'answered' by other voices from other positions" (*PDP* 88). This is true in theatre; it, too, includes several consciousnesses answerable to other positions. Critical of Bakhtin, Graham Pechey observes that to "imply even by omission that drama escaped this process [of dialogization] is to reflect unfavorably on that powerfully destabilising force that Bakhtin's more general case claims for the novel."[6] In theatre, gestures and utterances are dialogized, and as such they deserve attention within dramatic theory.

Notwithstanding the polemic concerning Bakhtin's relationship to drama, this essay will attempt to show that his dialogism is of value to dramatic theory. My purpose here is to compare, contrast, and critically reflect on two critiques of dramatic literature: dialectics and dialogics. After an account of the two theories—their similarities and differences—I will take up two paradigm dramas that will help illuminate the reasoning behind these critiques. The dramas, August Wilson's *The Piano Lesson* and Ntozake Shange's *for colored girls who have considered suicide/when the rainbow is enuf*, epitomize dialectic and dialogic drama, respectively. My analysis is intended to provide a deeper understanding of dialectics and dialogics in their relationship to dramatic literature and theory. In calling attention to plays that fall into the dialectical or dialogical subgenre, I hope to shed light on two predom-inant dramatic theories that embrace a wide variety of dramas. Dramatic theory can draw from Bakhtin's dialogics on the basis of polyphony, heteroglossia, and intertextuality, but drama can also give a qualified nod to dialectics on the basis of its methodological and epistemological contributions.

Defining Dialogics and Dialectics

Katerina Clark and Michael Holquist claim that Bakhtin "emphasizes performance, history, actuality, the openness of dialogue, as opposed to the closed dialectic of Structuralism's binary oppositions. Bakhtin makes the enormous leap from dialec-tical, or partitive, thinking, which is still presumed to be the universal norm, to dialogic or relational thinking." Clark and Holquist add that the difficulty posed by Bakhtin's dialogic theory "is to avoid thinking from within an all-pervasive si-multaneity without at the same time falling into the habit of reducing everything to a series of binary oppositions: not a dialectical either/or, but a dialogic both/and."[7]

For the purposes of dramatic theory, the difference between dialogics and dialectics is as follows: if the dialectical model is primarily adversarial, with conflict between ideas leading to synthesis, then the dialogic model presupposes as its goal a polyphony, or multiplicity of voices, voices not in conflict with each other, but instead sharing the same rhetorical space. Dialectics require binary opponents arriving at metaphysical reconciliation; dialogics, like atoms, collide, respond, and rebound off one another in an endless give and take. Bakhtin confirms as much when he says that dialogics in Dostoevsky's novels are worlds and ideas that are in no sense present "as links in a unified dialectical sequence, as stages along the path in the evolution of a unified spirit" (*PDP* 25). To be unified dialectically, Bahktin maintains, each novel "would form a completed philosophical whole, structured according to the dialectical method." The ultimate link in the dialectic, he says, "would inevitably turn out to be the author's synthesis" (*PDP* 25–26). Instead, as Holquist asserts, Bakhtin's dialogism is a defense of "the very capacity to have consciousness [that] is based on *otherness*. This otherness is not merely a dialectical alienation on its way to a sublation that will endow it with a unifying identity in higher consciousness. On the contrary, in dialogism consciousness *is* otherness." Holquist offers the following clarification:

> Dialogism's drive to meaning should not be confused with the Hegelian im-pulse toward a single state of higher consciousness in the future. In Bakhtin there is no *one* meaning being striven for: the world is a vast congeries of contesting meanings, a heteroglossia so varied that no single term capable of unifying its diversifying energies is possible.[8]

Along these lines, Gary Saul Morson and Caryl Emerson maintain that in dialogics we should not "expect some 'synthesis' or 'merging' of points of view: dialogue is not a self-consuming artifact, nor is it 'dialectic,' for dialectics (in the Hegelian or Marxist sense) can be contained within a single consciousness and overcomes contradictions in a single, monologic view." By contrast, they underscore that "in 'a dialogic encounter of two cultures . . . each retains its own unity and *open* totality, but they are mutually enriched.'"[9]

Bakhtin sees dialogics as antithetical to dialectics. He describes dialectics as follows:

> Take a dialogue and remove the voices (the partitioning of voices); remove the intonation (emotional and individualizing ones); carve out abstract con-cepts and judgments from living words and responses, [then] cram every-thing into one abstract consciousness—and that's how you get dialectics.[10]

This "recipe" for dialectics reflects on the Hegelian view of synthesis. As a result, writes Simon Dentith, Bakhtin rejects dialectics, "for the dialectic is a way of recognizing conflict and contradiction only to resolve them ultimately."[11]

I think the above comparisons of dialectics and dialogics are clear but incomplete; they provide some basic points of comparison between the two theoretical approaches, but they do not incorporate subtle distinctions. It is surely correct to say that Bakhtin lacks Hegel's faith in unifying principles. In rejecting Hegelian dialectics, Bakhtin makes it clear that human consciousness is at its *fullest* only when it is in relationship with another, when the give-and-take of dialogue, utterances, and responses, what he calls "answerability," operates communicatively. In *Toward a Philosophy of the Act*, he makes the point that unity closes human consciousness, while answerability expands it:

> The closer one moves to theoretical unity (constancy in respect of content or recurrent identicalness), the poorer and more universal is the actual uniqueness; the whole matter is reduced to the unity of content, and the ultimate unity proves to be an empty and self-identical possible content. The further individual uniqueness moves away from theoretical unity, the more concrete and full it becomes. . . .[12]

Where I take issue with the division between dialectics and dialogics is that it ignores the significant fact that during the 1840s a group of intellectuals, literary scholars, and philosophers dubbed the Young Hegelians (the young Karl Marx among them) had also challenged the Hegelian emphasis on synthesis. For the Young Hegelians, a dialectical worldview was conflictual, but they rejected reconciliation or unity; for them, dialectics remained in a state of unresolved tension. In fact, Bakhtin, according to Peter Zima, was influenced by the Young Hegelians. Zima asserts that Bakhtin's Young Hegelian aesthetics were manifest in his belief in the disruption of "the harmonious totality of Hegelian classicism," supplanting it with "disharmony, antinomy, and polyphony." Zima claims that, like the Young Hegelians and Nietzsche, Bakhtin chooses ambivalence, the openness of which cannot be curbed by Hegel's *Aufhebung*, or synthesis. He thus rejects the systematic dialectic of Hegel, whose aspiration toward total knowledge and the Absolute Idea is well-known, and develops an open, negative dialectic, which admits both the unity of the opposites and concept of mediation (*Vermittlung*) but not *Aufhebung* as a positive synthesis.

Bakhtin, as Zima makes clear, had much in common with the Young Hegelians. According to Zima, Bakhtin "starts from the dialectical unity of opposites, but he no longer believes in the possibility of a Hegelian '*Aufhebung*' and the construction of the historical system. The latter is abandoned, along with subject-object identity, Hegelian monologue, and Hegel's notion of truth, as a relic of classicism."[13]

We have, then, two aesthetics—Young Hegelian dialectics and Bakhtinian dialogics—that manifest similar characteristics. Both repudiate synthesis, reconciliation, and unity, rejecting the effort to bring drama to resolution or closure. In the final analysis, however, they diverge on matters of conflict, otherness, and answerability. According to the Young Hegelians, dialectical drama valorizes the binary features of conflict, with contrasting pairs of ideas clashing in opposition. It holds two oppositional positions in tension simultaneously, focusing on their antinomy through irony and conflict. As the Young Hegelians adopted Hegelian dialectics, they argued that conflict of ideas remained unresolved, i.e., they accepted the thesis-antithesis portion of Hegel's dialectic, but deleted synthesis. Nonetheless, the thesis-antithesis duality depends on a collision of ideologies for self-definition, with character points of view clarified and strengthened through conflict.

Bakhtin shares with the Young Hegelians an interest in character at least to the extent that discourse becomes ideological, expressing relations of social significance. However, he parts company with them in his emphasis on the dialogue itself as a condition of otherness, in which characters *become*, i.e., they take shape through discourse with another. Subjectivity surfaces through dialogue, through a process of becoming—coming into identity via a dialogic exchange—rather than ready-made characteristics already formed *before* dialogue happens. Character and consciousness are formed by responsiveness and answerability to others, and utterances are means through which communicative exchanges function. As David Danow contends, "the other assists in the ongoing process of determining the self, which also means determining the word of the self."[14] Character is, therefore, a fluid identity, codependent on speaking and listening. According to Bakhtin: "To be means to communicate dialogically. When dialogue ends, everything ends" (*PDP* 252).

Dialectics, as the Young Hegelians would have it, is confrontational, positing a clash of ideals without resolution. Characters come into being through conflict. Dialogics is different in that it opens events to a plethora of meanings and discourses that are not so much conflictual as they are circulatory. Ideas represented in utterances move around each other through dialogue, sometimes clashing, sometimes not, but never submerging into a unified field of vision. Dialogics does not privilege conflict as the sole means of difference; rather, it actively pursues cultural and individual *differences*—otherness—through dialogue, without depending on conflict. Rather than confrontation, Bakhtin emphasizes answerability, what he calls the values we inculcate "to every self-manifestation on the part of those around us."[15] We answer, respond, interact, and exchange ideas and utterances through negotiability, through the moment of interactive contact. This sense of acknowledging the outsidedness of the world (*vnenakhodimost'*) is, in Bakhtin's view, an active cocreation of personalities and images that links each person as a respondent to his or her reality and to other consciousnesses. Emerson rightly points out that for Bakhtin, what makes an individual whole "is a *response*."[16] And for Bakhtin, responding is manifested in words, dialogue, and utterances that embody numerous meanings depending upon inflections, past usage, tonality, receptivity, etc. In short, language and communication bridge the space between human beings. Michael F. Bernard-Donals underscores this point, maintaining that in Bakhtin's philosophy he "sought God—or, perhaps more accurately, an experience that one could liken to that of the divine in the everyday—in the space between humans that might be bridged by the word, by utterance. This space can be bridged only through energy and communication."[17] As a result, living beings are "unfinalizable" (*nezavershimye*) because as long as they are alive, they are always in communication with others, always responding, answering, probing, questioning, and exchanging utterances and ideas. Living consciousness is always relational, always evolving, and always in dialogue. Bakhtin writes:

> I am conscious of myself and become myself only while revealing myself for another, through another, and with the help of another. The most important acts constituting self-consciousness are determined by a relationship toward another consciousness (toward a *thou*). . . . The very being of man (both external and internal) is the *deepest communion. To be* means to *communicate. . . .* To be means to be for another, and through the other, for oneself. A person has no internal sovereign territory, he is wholly and always on the boundary: looking inside himself, he looks *into the eyes of another with the eyes of another. . . .* I cannot manage without another, I cannot become myself without another; I must find myself in another by finding another in myself (in mutual reflection and acceptance). (*PDP* 287)

A comparison of Bakhtinian dialogism to the theories of mid-nineteenth-century Young Hegelians, in particular the theories of Friedrich Hebbel and Hermann Hettner, is particularly elucidating for dramatic theory. Below I will consider the Young Hegelian concept of the dialectical drama, evaluate Bakhtin's dialogism, and conclude with an analysis of two paradigmatic dramatic texts.

Dialectical Drama

Friedrich Hebbel (1813–63) and Hermann Hettner (1821–82) came of age in the 1840s, when the Young Hegelian movement was taking firm root. This period witnessed numerous transitions: a shift from Hegelian speculative philosophy and transcendentalism to a secular tradition of humanism, historicism, and *bürgerlichen Realismus;* from Romantic subjectivism to social consciousness; and from political radicalism to nationalism in the *Vormärz,* or pre-1848 Revolutionary period. The Young Hegelians were, on the whole, a disparate group; nevertheless, they exercised considerable collective influence over literary theory.[18] William Brazill observes that their chief significance "was in diffusing Hegel's thought, making it possible for others to accept parts of his philosophy without a commitment to its totality, and transforming his emphasis into historicism."[19] According to Jürgen Habermas, "Hegel inaugurated the discourse of modernity; the Young Hegelians permanently established it, that is, they freed the idea of a critique nourished on the spirit of modernity from the burden of the Hegelian concept of reason."[20]

However, shifts in Hegelian philosophy from abstract reason to concrete social history did not usher in a single new theory, but rather conflicting views emerged which added to an already fragmented ideological condition. The Young Hegelians were, as Wolfgang Eßbach reminds us, "an untypical group of intellectuals," whose presence epitomized "*a philosophical school, a political party, a journalistic bohemia, and an aesthetic sect.*"[21] They converted theory into practice, ideology into realpolitik, and abstract logic into historical realism. John Toews comments that because "theory was the comprehension of concrete existence," the primary political task of the Young Hegelians "was defined as public enlightenment, as the destruction of illusions and critical unveiling of the real human needs and interests previously hidden and distorted by these illusions."[22] As we shall see, Hebbel and Hettner were swept up in the project of moving Hegelian philosophy from abstractions to social science. Let us first consider Hegel's dialectic, then return to the Young Hegelians.

Hegel regards drama as the art form most representative of dialectics. The dramatic action of a play, he states, "is that of individuals in conflict with one another," and the ethical fortitude of each character "supports the course of action."[23] Within conflicts—that is, within the shifting give and take of dramatic tension based on the relationship between two opposing ethical claims—the Hegelian dialectic introduces the idea that opposites are in fact capable of being held together through a network of thought. Each agent is linked through a struggle to elevate, preserve, and simultaneously negate its opposite. Characters alter their tactics according to the ebb and flow of dramatic action, but they remain steadfast in their ethics and principles. These principles, moreover, must represent the highest ideals. Hegel explains that dramatic action "is not confined to the simple, undisturbed implementation of a certain purpose, but rather depends throughout on colliding circumstances, passions, and characteristics and leads therefore to actions and reactions, which in their turn make necessary a further resolution of struggle and conflict (*des Kampfs und Zwiespalts*)." As a result, he argues that "what we see before us are the definite ends of individualized purposes in living personalities and conflictual situations" (*Vorlusengen über die Ästhetik* 475–76). Dramatic action thus becomes a process of colliding forces embodied in the ethos and actions of stage characters.

Essential to the Hegelian dialectic is the relationship of the material to the

Spirit, or Thought (*Geist*). For Hegel, Spirit represents the culmination of human consciousness: its activity epitomizes both the annulment of opposing forces and recognition of contradictions, resulting in a progression of consciousnesses through the spirit. The very existence of an idea for Hegel signals an antagonistic condition, and that condition must be confronted by what opposes it. Eventually, conflict must be overcome via synthesis, sublation, and resolution, leading to an understanding of the underlying world spirit that ultimately transcends materiality.

Hegel held that to understand reality one must clarify thought as the highest reconciliation between the ideal and the real, with the mind being the unifying entity of all rational existence. But only when the mind could hold two opposing thoughts, or contradictory ideals, was the spirit flourishing. Hegel claimed that "spirit [is] the highest attainment . . . an advance not only to the *intuition*, but to the thought—the clear conception of itself."[24] He predicates his belief on reconciliation in history and dramatic art; he wants to preserve their wholeness and harmony. Thus, his concept of drama is bound up with monologism. Moreover, in Hegel's system, the individual is an instrument within a larger dialectical process, subservient to history's processes.[25]

For Hegel, confrontation is the core purpose of drama, but the conflict represents more than trivial arguments. The dialectic serves as a bridge to the universal spirit of Pure Thought, but only after characters have aligned themselves thematically with ideals of a higher purpose—whether religious, political, social, familial, or otherwise. "The feeling of reconciliation," writes Hegel, "stands over the pure fear and tragic sympathies; reconciliation endures in the tragedy through the observation of eternal justice" (*Vorlusengen über die Ästhetik* 526). Modern drama advances dialectically because, as Hegel observes, "drama does not disintegrate into an inwardness as the lyric, with an external sphere in opposition to it; rather, drama portrays both an inwardness and *this*, the outer realization" (*Vorlesungen über die Ästhetik* 477). Rather than withdrawing from conflict, drama's aesthetic power is found in such conflicts that are raised to an external and clear confrontation.

For Young Hegelians, particularly left wing Hegelians like Hebbel and Hettner, Hegel's philosophy was in need of correction. They claimed that everything Hegel proposed in drama was sound, except for the concept of reconciliation.[26] It is precisely the category of totality (Pure Thought), linked to Hegel's reduction of art to reconciliation and synthesis, that was challenged by the Young Hegelians. Thus, the resulting secularization of Hegelian philosophy has been widely identified as the basis of Young Hegelian polemics.[27] Simply put, the Young Hegelians rejected the metaphysical structure of Hegel's Absolute Spirit in synthesis, claiming that it eventually drew attention away from matters of concrete reality.

Hebbel was one of the first to incorporate the Hegelian dialectic into his dramas and dramatic theories. Drama, he claims, only exists "when it illustrates for us how the individual attains the form and central focus in the struggle between his personal volition and the general will of the world, which modifies and alters his act . . . and that, in so doing, [drama] clarifies for us the nature of all human action."[28] In another important essay Hebbel breaks from Hegel, arguing that the dialectical conflict of ideals is rooted in concrete, tangible reality, not abstract thought. Dialectical ideals in conflict, he states, are not "the allegorical dressing up of the idea, not at all the philosophical idea, but rather the dialectic must be transferred to the immediacy of life itself."[29] In this manner, Hebbel sought to strip Hegel's dialectic from the realm of the individual mind, and place it into the world of social relationships; rather than reconciliation, Hebbel argued for a tragic ending in resignation, death, or similar devices.

Hettner's criticism of Hegel was directed both against the abstract claims of an Hegelian absolute spirit and all similar claims made by idealism. His rejection of Hegelian speculative aesthetics was based on giving up the Hegelian dream of philosophical reconciliation of the real and the ideal, and surrendering the metaphysical dream of philosophical transcendence of epistemological ethics.[30] He did not find it possible to reconcile himself to Hegel's demand for an absolute spirit, nor did he conceive of tragedy in terms of humanity's conflict with the gods or fate, a conflict in which the protagonist of any drama was certain to lose. The sense of cosmic disruption that Hegel finds in classical tragedy implies that an absolute order (*absolutische Ordnung*) exists in order to be disturbed. For Hettner, such order is no longer relevant in a secular world; audiences must make sense of a world in which social structures have grown fragmented and alien to the individual.

Hettner believed that the task of tragic drama is to shed light on the deteriorated and dysfunctional elements within society, remain on the concrete level throughout, and not diverge to the mind or spiritual matters. Tragedy arising from modern drama, Hettner says, is not achieved from superficial conflicts between enemies, the appearance of fate, or the arbitrariness of deus ex machina; rather, "the tragic struggle will be portrayed from the dialectics of principles of these ethical contrasts (*principiellen Dialektik dieser sittlichen Gegensätze*)."[31] Hettner, like Hebbel (and Bakhtin), advances the genre of ideas, in which drama captures internal conflict through competing idealistically motivated ethical principles.

The Young Hegelians borrowed from Hegel the principle that dialectics characterizes the manner in which a concept stands in relation to its opposite: the concept "lives" by generating its antithesis. However, they were not at all comfortable with Hegel's emphasis on resolution and a return to a higher, pure thought. They agreed with Hegel that the conflict's dialectical separation objectified the dramatic contrast, thereby blurring personal and egoistic aspects which might favor one side over another, but they did not accept Hegel's speculative philosophy, placing little significance on the concept of sublation. Like Hegel, they articulated a desire to find a way of establishing differences within dramatic structure. For them the dialectic was an inescapable conflict with no possible soteriology or reconciliation; what therefore remains from Hegel's dialectic is his "method." The process which begins with abstract categories or ideas and moves toward the concrete was simply a method by which playwrights come to grasp circumstances within which character interaction takes place. Thus, drama exists at the corporeal level, in the blood of its characters and in the passion of their ideals. In Young Hegelian dialectical drama, stage characters exhibit thought and passion in concrete reality rather than submitting to abstraction.

Bakhtinian Dialogism

Bakhtin shared with the Russian Formalists a concern for literary process, linguistics, and formalist structures in literature, but he departed from them in his emphasis on the way utterances shift meaning depending on the social forces that influence language.[32] For him, the way in which social and philosophical contexts define the meaning of utterances led to an emphasis on the heteroglossia of language: words and dialogue put into play, particularly in selected novels, have a multiplicity of meanings depending on the interaction of voices, not only in their dialogic exchange between people, but in the way words are deployed in temporal, spatial, and cultural contexts. Communication is not simply a matter of decoding words; it is a complex process that involves context, social relationships, and communion. Rather than containing a normative, centralized stratification of meaning where words remain static, utterances in active, daily usage change meaning as they refer to, and respond to, both alternative utterances in the immediate present, and the way utterances have been used in the past. In this way, the relationship between utterances is dialogic: words "dialogue" with other words, with the past, and with the social contexts. Dialogic utterances, he says, are "ideologically saturated," operating in the "midst of heteroglossia." At any given moment, utterances are active participants in "living heteroglossia," and this "determines the linguistic profile and style of the utterance to no less a degree than its inclusion in any normative centralizing system of a unitary language" (DI 271, 272). We can ascertain Bakhtin's value to dramatic literature by first illuminating his theories of history, philosophy, ethics, and literature.

Bakhtin maintains that history is metaphorically an architectonic movement akin to music, in which human thinking ebbs and flows in an "aestheticized, rhythmic process."[33] Rather than conflict leading to reconciliation, as Hegel would have it, history for Bakhtin is a mosaic of texts, a patchwork quilt of intertextuality, what Julia Kristeva calls Bakhtin's polyphony of ideas "written and read within the infrastructure of texts."[34] Texts adapt and absorb other texts, but rather than sublation, texts dialogue with each other; as a result, history is a textual discourse, a process of dialogue, exchange, and communal thought. Simply put, Hegel views history as a process of ideas that ultimately lead, in a linear way, to a perfect union of the individual and the state; Bakhtin's view is democratic, permitting voices to flourish in a continuous and circular exchange of ideas.

Bakhtin's philosophical theory of dialogism maintains that there are essentially three levels of dialogics in literature: the philosophical relationship between the Self and Other, the interaction of dialogue between characters in the novel, and the relationship that binds one utterance to another through intertextuality. In the first instance, Bakhtin positions the relationship between the Self and Other, or the Self and Object (Things), as a way around the Kantian rift between the Self and the World. Bakhtin starts from Kant's position that all human knowledge begins with the nature of appearances and the reliance on subjective unity of a priori reason, intuition, and imagination that are grounded in assumptions (generalities), but proceeds to analyze the realm of consciousness from a slightly different approach. He posits what Daelemans and Maranhão call the architectonic, or bridging activities of the mind that "partake in a dialogue that is influenced by the *hic et nunc* characteristics of the most immediate reality."[35]

The mind for Bakhtin is in dialogue with the world through time and space, and this exchange fosters consciousness. Consciousness is therefore never independent, transcendental, or constructed on a priori categories as Kant would have it, but rather it is constructed on a level of communication, grounded in the particularities of life as communications proceed temporally and spatially. As a result, Bakhtin emphasizes dialogue as a critical and essential tool in building consciousness. He explains:

> The dialogic nature of consciousness [is] the dialogic nature of human life itself. The single adequate form for *verbally expressing* authentic human life is the *open ended dialogue*. Life by its very nature is dialogic. To live means to participate in dialogue: to ask questions, to heed, to respond, to agree, and so forth. (*PDP* 293)

Bakhtin's philosophical attempt to turn Kantian transcendental aesthetics into living reality bears similarities to the way in which Young Hegelians turned Hegel's dialectics into materiality, and ultimately into a realism of sorts.[36] Both Bakhtin and the Young Hegelians wanted to "ground" abstractions in everyday life. Bakhtin's central concern, notes Lisa Eckstrom, was "to ground Kant's categorical imperative in the particulars and concreteness of an individual life."[37] Holquist adds to this, noting that for Bakhtin "Kant was right to emphasize the central role of time/space categories in perception, but he was wrong to locate perception in some transcendent, *general* consciousness."[38] Bakhtin's idea of the chronotope, what he calls the "intrinsic connectedness of temporal and spatial relationships that are artistically expressed in literature" (*DI* 84), is not transcendental, but lives in the specific, immediate present of the lived experiential world, i.e., in the *historical moment*. And the moment is not fixed but fluid; history is not a disembodied entity, but rather is flexible, protean, and malleable. Our perception of it changes as the future unfolds.

Bakhtin worked through Kant's problematic—the permanent inaccessibility of things in themselves—by emphasizing the concreteness of dialogue. Active communication places a significant emphasis on utterances; language as the prime means of communication can bridge the gulf between the Self and Others (the inability of knowing things in themselves) and supply the building blocks for consciousness. Without dialogue and the focus on another, consciousness for Bakhtin is never fully formed. Holquist stresses the fact that in dialogism, "the very capacity to have consciousness is based on *otherness*," and that it "cannot be stressed enough that for him [Bakhtin] 'self' is dialogic, a relation."[39] Kant's split between mind and world is bridged for Bakhtin not through self-conscious categories and synthesis, but through architectonics, through bridgeable constructions of dialogue saturated in answerability, intertextuality, and utterances.

Bakhtin's neo-Kantian theories were based on his relationship to Hermann Cohen and the Marburg School of thought.[40] According to Holquist and Clark, Cohen and the German Marburg theorists popularly received in Bakhtin's Russian circles stressed the need to overcome the gap "between reason and belief, metaphysics and theology," and that Bakhtin's career "may be thought of as part of this ongoing attempt to bring philosophy somehow into congruence with theology." The ethical concerns which were to occupy much of Bakhtin's philosophy—the bridge, or architectonics, between mind and world, one individual to another— can be said to have a direct relationship to Cohen's preoccupation with humanity and God. Bakhtin, however, transferred ethical concerns from Cohen's theology to the reality of language. As Holquist and Clark maintain, Bakhtin sought God "in the space between men that could be bridged by the word, by utterances. Instead of seeking God's place in stasis and silence, Bakhtin sought it in energy and communication."[41]

For Bakhtin, dialogue was the basis for ethical claims: because no one lives in isolation, each human being is ethically "answerable" to others. His ethics of answerability argues, moreover, that human values are not preconceived and ready made (*gotovyi*), but are constructed, and come to fruition, through dialogue.[42] Thus, there is always a surplus (*izbytok*), or synergy of values, each conceived in the process of communicating with other values. Moreover, no value (or voice) is privileged, but rather each is unique yet answerable to another value. Ethical values address other values, and evolve accordingly. Bernard-Donals asserts that the human capacity for reaction to values "is what Bakhtin calls 'addressivity.'" Individuals react and relate to the physical world, and this relationship, Bernard-Donals adds, "is directly related to Bakhtin's neo-Kantian origins: the mind must have some kind of relationship to those things exterior to it."[43] As humans relate, they formulate ethics. In the case of literature, ethical values are equally distributed between the author and the characters. Thus, characters "answer" each other's values dialogically, with the author taking a seat alongside the "other" characters. For Bakhtin, the "unity of answerability" enables both self-reflection and "responsibility" to share space and time in the world. Answerability, he says, "entails guilt, or liability to blame. It is not only mutual answerability that art and life must assume, but also mutual liability to blame." Because we live in this world, ethical responsibility means sharing the guilt and blame for the action of others. He goes on to say that art and life are not one, but rather "they must become united in myself—in the unity of my answerability."[44] Only when author, character, and reader engage in dialogue can answerability function.

Utterances are the key concept to which the concentric notions of dialogism and answerability adhere. Words not only carry within themselves the intentionality of the speaker and the interpretation of the listener, but they also carry within them preceding usage, and as a result, no utterance, says Tzvetan Todorov, "is devoid of the intertextual dimension."[45] The basis of Bakhtinian dialogism is founded on the intertextual nature of utterances. This intertextual relationship has three components: speaker, listener, and what Todorov calls "the things themselves [that] have been touched, at least in one of their previous states, by other discourses that one cannot fail to encounter."[46] Bakhtin explains that any utterance always has an addressee (of various sorts, with varying degrees of proximity, concreteness, awareness, and so forth), whose responsive understanding the author of the speech work seeks and surpasses. But in addition to this addressee (the second party), the author of the utterance, with a greater or lesser awareness, presupposes a higher *superaddressee* (third), whose absolutely just responsive understanding is presumed, either in some metaphysical distance or in a distant historical time (the loophole addressee).[47]

This inventory of discourse establishes intertextuality, giving utterances themselves a plurality of meanings and ideologies. The utterance, Rick Bowers informs us, "is always formed in relation to the other and is therefore ripe with communicative possibilities, with intentions for dialogic interaction." Such interaction, Bowers contends, facilitates the mutual interaction of speaker, utterance, and hearer all in unfixed dialogical relationship to each other. Communication begins as a two-way interaction, then multiplies. Dialogism represents the innate condition of all utterance.[48]

Bakhtin's definition of dialogism as a "plurality of independent and unmerged voices and consciousnesses, a genuine polyphony of fully valid voices" was found to be "the chief characteristic of Dostoevsky's novels" (*PDP* 6). This polyphony of voices in Dostoevsky's literature maintains several consciousnesses in one unit, or novel. Whereas monologism is a communicative mode in which the author's presence is foregrounded, dialogism "was capable of representing someone else's idea, preserving its full capacity to signify as an idea, while at the same time also preserving a distance, neither confirming the idea nor merging it with [the author's] own expressed ideology" (*PDP* 85). Dialogics is, as Lynne Pearce tells us, "predicated on the active communication of two participants: the speaker and his or her addressee,"[49] which, in the novel, bolsters the philosophic nature of dialogue. As such, dialogics can only be grasped, as Terry Eagleton suggests, "in terms of its inevitable orientation towards another."[50]

What Bakhtin insisted on is a literary truth found in the sign that "requires a plurality of consciousnesses" (*PDP* 81). Frank Farmer clarifies this point, asserting that in Bakhtinian perspective, dialogic truth is obliged to resist all those other versions of truth that, say, locate it *above* us (as in theological certitude), *outside* us (as in empirical "findings"), and *inside* us (as in Romantic and psychological constructions of essential discourses). What these various [other] *topoi* of knowledge share, Bakhtin might point out, are answers that neither require nor invite a response.[51]

But dialogic truth, since it is relational, *always requires a response;* it depends on answerability, communicative processes, and interrelationships of utterances that form the polyphony and heteroglossia of which he speaks.

Dialogics creates an interactive world of ideas and thoughts, without a dominant thought. Rather, a multiplicity of thoughts is evident. Bakhtin argues that what "Dostoevsky's characters say constitutes an arena of never-ending struggle with others' words, in all realms of life and creative ideological activity. For this reason these utterances may serve as excellent models of the most varied forms for transmitting and framing another's discourse" (*DI* 349). For Bakhtin, dialogics itself is an endless exchange "of social forces perceived not only in their static coexistence, but also as a dialogue of different times, epochs, and days, a dialogue that is forever dying, living, being born: coexistence and becoming are here fused into an indissoluble concrete unity that is contradictory, multi-speeched, and heterogeneous." It is dialogics "in their openendedness, their inability to say anything once and for all or to think anything through to its end," that creates "their lifelike concreteness, their 'naturalistic quality'" (*DI* 365).

Dialogics rejects dialectics, even Young Hegelian dialectics, because dialogics affirms a Bakhtinian polyphony of voices, rather than the Young Hegelian emphasis on contradictory, or opposing utterances. For Bakhtin, the Hegelian dialectic is monological, and so unacceptable, while the dialectic of the Young Hegelians is rejected because it relies solely on confrontation. In confrontation, the antagonists are held together in a unified field of vision consisting of oppositional claims, even if they fail to resolve them. Young Hegelian drama emphasizes the need of one agent to attempt to obviate the other's ideology. Bakhtin rejects this antagonistic binarism, preferring to see characters as unfinished (*nezaversben*), proclaiming a style akin to an open plane, where voices collide like atoms:

Where others saw a single thought, he [Dostoevsky] was able to find and feel out two thoughts, a bifurcation; where others saw a single quality, he discovered in it the presence of a second and contradictory quality. . . . In every voice he could hear two contending voices, in every expression a crack, and the readiness to go over immediately to another contradictory expression; in every gesture he detected confidence and lack of confidence simultaneously; he perceived the profound ambiguity, even multiple ambiguity, of every phenomenon. But none of these contradictions and bifurcations ever became dialectical. . . . [T]hey were, rather, spread out in a plane, as standing alongside or opposite one another, as consonant but not merging or as hopelessly contradictory, as an eternal harmony of unmerging voices or as their unceasing and irreconcilable quarrel. (*PDP* 30)

Bakhtin's dialogics is an ethics of answerability and a respect for Otherness. Thus, dialogics unfolds the notion of Self addressing and answering an Other, rather than the Self in conflict with, or trying to obviate, an Other. On an ethical level, this distinguishes dialogics from Young Hegelian dialectics, where the Self is manifest in self-consciousness (preformed notions of identity), with the appearance of consciousness brought forth in conflict. In contrast, Bakhtin's dialogics emphasize intertextuality over individuality; context (heteroglossia) over competing texts; and linguistic hybridity (polyglossia) over antagonism. Bakhtinian dialogue calls attention to the presence of meaning as lying outside the subject's consciousness; consciousness is determined not from the immediate clash of the subject's volition in conflict (as Hegel and the Young Hegelians would have it), but from the subject's relationships to, and communication with, a multitude of levels.

Paradigm Texts

August Wilson's *The Piano Lesson* (1987) and Ntozake Shange's *for colored girls who have considered suicide/when the rainbow is enuf* (1976) may serve as models of dialectical and dialogical case studies, respectively. In Wilson's play, the conflict between siblings for control of the family piano is more than one of mere possession; for each the piano symbolizes differing ideals. The conflict of interest rises above mere sibling rivalry, becoming instead ideological conflicts based on ethical claims. In Shange's play, the seven characters are voices whose dialogic exchange epitomizes heteroglossia and polyphony. The characters speak to us and to each other, sometimes in inner conflict, other times in commiseration with each other, but always in what Bakhtin calls the "spirit of this world in the state of becoming" (*PDP* 19). Shange creates an interactive world of ideas and voices, without an overriding, dominant, or authorial presence. The discourse in *for colored girls* is situated in a multiplicity of voices, what Bakhtin describes in Dostoevsky's novels as the mode of *"coexistence* and *interaction"* (*PDP* 28).

In the first play, *The Piano Lesson,* Wilson sets the stage for a dialectic confrontation of ethical values between Boy Willie and his sister, Berniece. The plot revolves around the return of Boy Willie from the South to Pittsburgh, ostensibly to sell his watermelons, but actually to reclaim the family heirloom, the piano. Boy Willie wants to sell the piano so that he can raise funds to buy land in the South. Berniece opposes the sale of the piano, because for her the instrument represents the spirit of her ancestors. Their great-grandfather had carved his artwork into the piano, making it not only an instrument of music, but also an object of family value. Moreover, their father died trying to regain possession of it. For Boy Willie, the sale of the piano can help raise enough money for a return to the South and to buy the property once owned by Sutter, the white slave owner whose family also had owned the piano in question. But Berniece will not allow her brother to sell it, defending her half of the inheritance. Although she has not played the piano for many years out of fear that it is haunted (which it is, by Sutter), still she clings to it as symbolic of the family's heritage.

The Piano Lesson represents a dialectical conflict of ethical principles. As the Young Hegelians would have it, the play represents two competing voices with equally valid yet incompatible claims that create the dramatic conflict. Devon Boan reminds us that the "action of the play is driven by conflict over how best to engage history—as iconographically centered mythology, which would celebrate the *events* of the past, or as foundation for the present, which would seek to fulfill its *promise.*"[52] For Wilson, black history is rooted in the African continuum *and* in slavery. Africa is home, but the South is, for Wilson, where blacks tilled, toiled, and created; to consider the South as insignificant is to reject not only the roots of Negro spirituals, the blues, and the oral tradition, but the rightful ownership of the land itself. Boy Willie's desire to own land represents the ethical view of black entitlement to roots in the land that held them captives. Boy Willie says as much in the following monologue:

> I take my hat off whenever somebody say my daddy's name. But I ain't gonna be no fool about no sentimental value. You can sit up here and look at the piano for the next hundred years and it's just gonna be a piano. . . . Now I want to get Sutter's land with that piano. I get Sutter's land and I can go down and cash in the crop and get my seed. . . . Cause that land give back to you. I can make me another crop and cash that in. . . . But that piano don't put out nothing else. . . . Now, the kind of man my daddy was he would have understood that.[53]

In contrast, Berniece's ethical position represents Africa, family, and tradition. According to August Wilson's biographer Sandra Shannon, Berniece "believes that the piano is a monument to her ancestors, which, by right, ought to be preserved."[54] Kim Pereira adds to this, saying that the masklike images on the piano record "the history of this family for several generations, imbuing the piano "with a totemic aura, for it now symbolizes the struggle of one family to survive slavery and sharecropping."[55] Berniece's response to Boy Willie in the following passage underscores her positionality and *fixed* view of the world:

> You ain't taking that piano out of my house.
> (*She crosses to the piano*)
> Look at this piano. Look at it. Mama Ola polished this piano with the tears for seventeen years. For seventeen years she rubbed on it till her hands bled. Then she rubbed the blood in . . . mixed it up with the rest of the blood on it. Every day that God breathed life into her body she rubbed and cleaned and polished and prayed over it.
> (*The Piano Lesson* 52)

The play, then, is a dialectical conflict of two righteous wills. Their struggle is manifested in the symbols of seed and blood: Boy Willie wants to plant seeds for the future in Southern roots, while Berniece longs to maintain blood ties to family and African roots. Both "seed" and "blood" are symbolic terms each character employs to bolster his/her ethical position; both characters are steeped in conceptions of moral fortitude and justice; and both characters *fix their identities to larger ethical claims, each of which is monologic.*

The dramatic structure revolves around this conflict, which epitomizes the *ready-made existence* of Boy Willie and Berniece. Their antagonism builds the inner tension of the play, and the conflict is such that the drama's focus underscores a dialectical movement. Moreover, the intended audience response should be to recognize the actions of both siblings as morally correct. In neo-Hegelian drama, audiences typically accept two opposing viewpoints, and in this way, as Hans-Georg Gadamer asserts, we learn in Hegelian terms to understand ourselves, meaning "that we sublate (*aufheben*) the discontinuity and atomism of isolated experiences in the continuity of our own existence."[56]

Bakhtin perceives this need for antagonism to be less creative, less interesting, and less profound than dialogic structure. The second play, Shange's *for colored girls*, is not so much a play about conflict as it is about the dialogic interaction of black women. The play is a dialogization because every word and gesture is, in Bakhtin's words, "open ended dialogue," in which characters participate "wholly and throughout [their] whole life: with [their] eyes, lips, hands, soul, spirit, and with [their] whole body and deeds" (*PDP* 293). Characters in *for colored girls* exhibit architectonic activities that are influenced by the *hic et nunc* characteristics of intertextual dialogue through Bakhtinian elements of dialogic utterances, polyphony of wills, and nonfinalizable structure.

In this play, Shange tells of the experiences of seven black women. The portrayal is accomplished through storytelling, dance, and poetic expression, what Shange calls a choreopoem. The characters recite, interact, and tell stories of their lives, but there is no feeling of contestation among competing wills. Seven women, dressed in the colors of the rainbow—yellow, red, green, purple, blue, and orange, with the addition of the color outside the rainbow, brown—sing, dance, and report significant events in their lives. The colors of the rainbow signify the polyphonic position of the characters: the various colors represent distinct, personalized voices and individuals whose ideological discourse is separate and independent. Though all the women share their experiences from the point of view of being women of color, they are unique, thus avoiding any authorial merging or ideological sublation.

The play asserts the uniqueness, individuality, and creativity of the characters: each tells about the abuses she experienced from men, about her discoveries of famous black historical figures, and about her friendships, losses, gains, and self-discoveries. As the Lady in Orange says:

> ever since I realized there waz someone callt
> a colored girl an evil woman a bitch or a nag
> I been tryin not to be that & leave bitterness
> in somebody else's cup /come to somebody to love me[57]

Earlier, the Lady in Brown articulates her liberation, declaring:

> sing a black girls song
> bring her out
> to know herself
> to know you
> but sing her rhythms
> carin/struggle/hard times
> sing her song of life
> she's been dead so long
> closed in silence so long
> she doesn't know the sound
> of her own voice
>   (*for colored girls* 2–3)

In both an aesthetic and ethical way, Shange's *rainbow of colors* is comparable to Bakhtin's *polyphony of voices*. Each color, or voice, *becomes* through dialogue, answers and responds to other utterances, and the juxtaposition of colors/voices enables us to view the varied hues/tones of their humanity. Each color/voice answers the other, creating an intertextual collage that both dialogues with the Other and constructs consciousness. The importance of revealing color in the play's dialogue echoes Bakhtin's often quoted magnanimous expression of self-construction: "I am conscious of myself and become myself only while revealing myself for another, through another, and with the help of another. The most important acts constituting self-consciousness are determined by a relationship toward another consciousness" (*PDP* 287).

Daelemans and Maranhão maintain that the combination of "'answerability' and the necessary 'architectonics' in building the bridge between Self and Other—conditions necessary for being 'in existence'—leads to an ethic of response-ability, in which 'we' are accountable for 'our' unique placement in existence."[58] For Bakhtin, answerability and responsibility lead to the construction of an axiological existence that fosters communal, rather than conflictual, values. Shange shares with Bakhtin the view that colors/voices evolve through *chronotopic*, or spatiotemporal conditions, allowing for a multiplicity of ethics that are never arranged hierarchically, but respond in time and space. Instead of fostering ethical competition (as in the case of *The Piano Lesson* and the conflict over the piano), Shange puts forth the idea that individuals are part of the chronotropic landscape and integral components of the rainbow.

Multiplicity, rather than conflict, forms the basis of the play. This multiplicity is not only represented by interactive voices, but also by revealing a dialogic polyphony beneath the surface. Shange, like Bakhtin, maintains that the beauty of a person lies not in her separateness—in her singularity of color—but in her relational and dialogic interaction with others. Shange:

> The rainbow is a fabulous symbol for me. If you see only one color, it's not beautiful. If you see them all, it is. A colored girl, by my definition, is a girl of many colors. But she can only see her overall beauty if she has to look deep within her.[59]

This beauty comes from the interactive respect of others, what Bakhtin might call "seeing the other whole," while maintaining one's self-respect and dignity. The vocal and gestural give and take, or call and response, of the characters serve as a paradigm of Bakhtinian dialogics.

All the characters come from outside the major urban centers of the United States; the *outsidedness* symbolizes their marginality, but also addresses Bakhtin's insistence on outsideness. For Bakhtin outsideness does not mean alienation, but rather what Emerson calls a "healthy self" that is "highly vulnerable and wholly involved in others." Emerson adds that the healthy self "does not pretend (in the name of empathy or devotion) to duplicate [the other's] particular space or time; it enters another's worldview and then, with a memory of that other horizon, returns to its own place. It must return, because only by that act does it regain its distinctive excess, or surplus, of vision vis-à-vis the other."[60] The women enter each other's worldview, see the other whole, learn from their interactive experiences, and return to their positionality healthier and more informed of their own existence not only as women of color, but as people.

Though the characters in *for colored girls* share a common experience of outsideness (living outside the mainstream), each character asserts uniqueness and individuality not only through a personal ideology expressed in dialogue, but through gesture as well. The incorporation of the other supports the feelings of community and multiple values, adding in Bakhtinian terms to the surplus of values. And the incorporation of dance as a gestural utterance underscores the various and multifaceted array of expressions; it adds to the diversity of utterances and bolsters the centrifugal force in language that refuses the unifying principle by operating in what Bakhtin calls "the midst of heteroglossia," or social diversity of speech (*DI* 271). Gesture highlights a character's ideology, permitting the audience to view individual complexities that alone cannot be captured by mere words. It can simultaneously contradict, augment, and support the verbal utterances, adding alternative and contradictory ideas, thus increasing the range of expression that ultimately destabilizes unity. And most important, gesture can significantly *dialogue* with another gesture, speaking through *body language* with another.

Gesture and movement have a polyphony of meanings for Shange. She explains that the "freedom to move in space, to demand of my own sweat a perfection that could continually be approached, though never known, waz poem to me, my body & mind ellipsing, probably for the first time in my life" (*for colored girls* xv). Her concept of drama accords with what Bakhtin describes as Dostoevsky's refusal to set in motion a text "along a temporal path or in an evolving sequence." Rather than linearity, Dostoevsky spreads out his dialogue "in a plane, as standing alongside or opposite one another, . . . as an eternal harmony of unmerging voices" (*PDP* 30). Dostoevsky conceives his novels as a world, Bakhtin says, "primarily in terms of space, not time" (*PDP* 28). Characters in Shange's play evolve spatially, through passion and gesture, as their voices create a polyphony of ideas. The dialogue and movement of the play move into what Bakhtin calls "the deepest molecular and ultimately, subatomic levels" (*DI* 300). In other words, voices and gestures move like atoms, circling, occasionally colliding, but nevertheless sharing space. According to Mae Gwendolyn Henderson, if "the psychic functions as an internalization of heterogeneous social voice, black women's speech/writing becomes at once dialogue between self and society and between self and psychic."[61] Like call and response patterns, the words in Shange's play also move outward, toward an intertextuality with other black female voices.[62] This intertextuality, what Kristeva calls textual "ambivalence," which implies "the insertion of history (society) into a text and of this text into history,"[63] resides in *for colored girls*. In Shange's play each character enters into a dialogue with the self, with the other, with the audience, and with society, providing the appropriate model for articulating both individuality and intertextuality.

The play moves back and forth between stories and interaction, drawing no unifying conclusions, making no overriding authorial statement, but instead celebrating the diversity of black women. Each character asserts her will, remaining *steadfast in her voice without merging into one thematic whole*. The final words of the play are a tribute to black women as people becoming, growing, and evolving: "& this is for colored girls who have considered suicide/but are movin to the ends of their own rainbows" (*for colored girls* 67).

There is a lack of finalizability to the events, reflecting the condition that Bakhtin calls "an openendedness, a living contact with unfinished, still evolving contemporary reality (the openended present)" (*DI* 7). In *for colored girls*, the ideas spoken by each character have not been hierarchized—the author's voice does not emerge on top. Rather, each character's ideas are deeply internalized, and their personalities are firmly rooted in the society of their times. Each character takes shape through dialogue and movement. The full portrayal of the characters is achieved by their physical and vocal discourse at the moment of contact in the theatre. This is similar to Bakhtin's notion that "*nothing conclusive has yet taken place in the world, the ultimate word of the world and about the world has not yet been spoken, the world is open and free, everything is still in the future and will always be in the future*" (*PDP* 166). Shange's play is a nonevent *until performed*. It is in an unfinished form, waiting until it is embodied by people, by actresses bringing their uniqueness to the role. Whereas *The Piano Lesson* lives in the intellectual ideas of dialectical conflict, and can be understood outside the moment of performance, *for colored girls* demands performance, living beings, for the creation of its meaning. It is dialogic in the purest sense, since its existence becomes manifest through dialogue, through the presence of voices/colors in a collage of sound and gesture.

In *for colored girls*, the world is open to an infinite array of possibilities through the freedom of word and movement. In the case of the word, Shange draws attention to the use of "stuff." In a lengthy address, the Lady in Green begins by saying:

somebody almost walked off wid alla my stuff
not my poems or a dance I gave up in the street
but somebody almost walked off wid alla my stuff

like a kleptomaniac workin hard & forgettin while
stealin
this is mine/this aint yr stuff
    (*for colored girls* 52)

The word *stuff,* as this speech reveals, has a polyphony of meanings; unlike Wilson's *seed* and *blood,* with its monolithic attention to African American heritage and specificity of meaning, *stuff* is ideologically saturated: the signifier and the thing signified are pulled apart. *Stuff* can mean belongings, things, and objects, but it can simultaneously mean identity, passions, and self-respect. As such, its multiplicity of meanings is, as V. N. Voloshinov asserts, *"the constitutive feature of word,"* and as a result, *"such a word, in essence, has virtually no meaning; it is all theme.* Its meaning is *inseparable from the concrete situation of its implementation."* Thus, Voloshinov claims that the theme of the word "is different each time, just as the situation is different each time."[64] It is a *living word* with a surplus of inferences, rich in nuance and parody, that cannot exist in a singular, or ideologically fixed way. *Stuff* exists, as Bakhtin might tell us, within heteroglossia, since "between the word and its object, between the word and the speaking subject, there exists an elastic environment of other alien words about the same subject, the same theme, and this environment is often difficult to perpetrate." It is in the process of living interaction with the specific environment, Bakhtin maintains, that "the word may be individualized and given stylistic shape."[65] *Stuff* exists only in the time and space of its presence before us and spoken by the actress; its meaning bends with time and space. Rather than a fixed ideology (as in *seed* and *blood*), *stuff* both parodies and exemplifies objects, things, possessions, and identity; it comments on, and simultaneously fosters self-respect. It maintains the dignity of the speaker who operates within a multitude of possibilities, and at the same time carries a self-referential parody that evokes humor.

Holquist draws attention to Bakhtin's dialogism that has particular relevance to Shange and Wilson. He explains that dialogism "is a philosophy of the trees as opposed to a philosophy of the forest: it conceives society as a simultaneity of uniqueness."[66] Shange, likewise, is a philosopher of the trees: for her, African Americans are unique individuals of differing colors/voices. Wilson, in contrast, is a philosopher of the forest: for him, the whole canopy of African American culture is fundamentally held together—rooted and finalized—by a dialectical conflict between *seed* (Boy Willie's desire to plant and farm in the South) and *blood* (African roots and the blood of Mama Ola). In *The Piano Lesson,* the ready-made and finalized characters come prepared to defend their ethical positions; their positions are unimpeachable, and the dialogue merely reveals their conflict. Their words are fixed, which is to say that the themes underlying *seed* and *blood* are rigid codes that signify their specific and respective symbolic referents. For Bakhtin and Shange, dialogism is open ended, a never ending emphasis on the multiple meaning of words that, like people, are not finalizable. They reject Structuralism's ideological unity of signifier to the thing signified, opting instead for a world that, as Morson and Emerson maintain, "clusters and unclusters."[67] Words are not merely conversation tools or weapons that defend ethical claims; rather, as Emerson explains, what interested Bakhtin was not so much the social fact of several people exchanging words with one another in a room as it was the idea that each word contains within itself diverse, discriminating, often contradictory "talking" components. The more often a word is used in speech acts, the more contexts it accumulates and the more its meanings proliferate. Utterances do not forget. And by their very nature, they resist unity and homogenization—two states that Bakhtin, a close student of biology, considered akin to death.[68]

Likewise, the word *stuff*: the more often it is repeated in time and space, the more context it accumulates and the more its meaning expands. The multiple meanings of the word create a surplus, or synergy of values, since each potential meaning borrows and interacts with the previous usages and meanings.

The themes expressed in *for colored girls* reflect the importance of ideas in continuous interaction; the play stresses otherness, dialogue, and multiple views. Black women are not a monolithic group whose aims and desires are unified in a single vision; rather, the play presents black women in their differentiation and individuality within a community. Holquist describes Bakhtin's view on this point: "Since Bakhtin places so much emphasis on otherness, and on otherness defined precisely as other *values*, community plays an enormous role in his thought. Dialogism is, among other things, an exercise in social theory."[69] Shange's play is a community event, a social theory in practice, one which brings seven black women together in a *dialogic play of utterances*. Each character expresses her volition through dialogue; but at no time is this will submerged, sublated, or synthesized. Nor is it brought into view through conflict with each other. Rather, each volition becomes clear in its differentiation, in its contrast to others. Moreover, only in the event itself, in the performance, are the utterances of ideology gathered together. Bakhtin emphasizes the fact that "the artistic will of polyphony is a will to combine many wills, a will to the event" (*PDP* 21). Clark and Holquist make clear that Bakhtin's concept of creation means that one must

> "live into" an other's consciousness; I see the world through that other's eyes. But I must never completely meld with that version of things, for the more successfully I do so, the more I will fall prey to the limitations of the other's horizon. A complete fusion (a dialectical *Aufhebung*) even were it possible, would preclude the difference required by dialogue.[70]

Shange's nonlinear play contains no narrative movement per se; rather, it is a plurality of discourses. Voices enter into dialogue with each other, share commonality, but never lose individuality; voices thus maintain a level of democratic interaction. John Timpane calls attention to the democratic nature of the play: in *for colored girls*, characters "speak for themselves as centered personas, and at other times they narrate or act out the lives of others. In this second function it is always clear that they are bearers of someone else's tale." Shange, Timpane explains, "insists on the rough edges, the open, the fragment" that conveys a "distinctly democratic" presentation of wills firmly in the "tradition of the democracy . . . as described by Bakhtin."[71] For Bakhtin, dialogics means the democratic exchange of voices that both represent someone else's ideas and maintain one's own. The same can be said of Shange: the *rainbow of voices* in the play are unique, capable of signifying ideas, able to move confidently into another space (literally and figuratively), while simultaneously preserving a distance between self and other.

We conclude, then, that there are differences between dialectics and dialogics, but they do not lie primarily in their respective attitudes toward synthesis. It is not true, as we have seen, that all dialectics respect wholeness as Bakhtin understood (and rejected) it. Rather, the difference between Young Hegelian dialectics and Bakhtin's dialogics lies in their approach toward resolution and otherness. For the Young Hegelians, the endless struggle of differences underscores dramatic action. For dialogics, the play of voices results in a multiplicity of performances. For both, unity is deleted; but in dialogics, an openness and willingness for an entity or character to embrace other ideas without merging itself into a single idea creates the most desirable theoretical framework for drama.

Notes

1. Marvin Carlson, "Theater and Dialogism," *Critical Theory and Performance*, Janelle G. Reinelt and Joseph Roach, eds. (Ann Arbor: University of Michigan Press, 1992), 313–23; Helene Keyssar, "Drama and the Dialogic Imagination: *The Heidi Chronicles and Fefu and Her Friends*," *Modern Drama* 34.1 (March 1991): 88–106. A number of essays and books deal with Bakhtin's carnivalesque and the theatre, in particular, Michael D. Bristol, *Carnival and Theatre: Plebian Culture and the Structure of Renaissance England* (London: Methuen), 1985. Also, Graham Pechey deals briefly with Bakhtin and drama in his "On the Borders of Bakhtin: Dialogisation, Decolonisation," *Bakhtin and Cultural Theory*, Ken Hirschkop and David Shepard, eds. (Manchester: Manchester University Press, 1989), 39–67 (see especially 57–62).

2. I am inclined to agree with René Wellek's assertion that although Dostoevsky's novels contain "independent voices which become subjects in their own right and do not serve the ideological position of the author," Bakhtin is "simply wrong if he pushes this view so far as to deny the authorial voice of Dostoevsky." In Wellek, *A History of Modern Criticism: 1750–1950* Vol. 7 (New Haven: Yale University

Press, 1991), 357. Henryk Markiewicz adds to this, noting that "Dostoevsky's novels are less polyphonic than Bakhtin would wish them to be." In Markiewicz, "Polyphony, Dialogism and Dialectics: Bakhtin's Theory of the Novel," *Literary Criticism and Theory* Vol. I, Joseph P. Strelka, ed. (Bern: Peter Lang, 1984), 446. It may be that Bakhtin's significance lies in his theory of polyphony, and less so in his analysis of Dostoevsky's novels. This issue, however, is too broad a topic to cover here. Suffice it to say, I will draw from Bakhtin's theory of dialogism, not his analysis of Dostoevsky's novels.

3. Bakhtin, *Problems of Dostoevsky's Poetics*, Caryl Emerson, tr. (Minneapolis: University of Minnesota Press, 1984), 17. Future references will be listed as *PDP* and page number in the text.

4. Bakhtin, "Discourse in the Novel," *The Dialogic Imagination: Four Essays*, Caryl Emerson and Michael Holquist, eds. (Austin: University of Texas Press, 1981), 266. Future references to this work will be listed as *DI* and page number in the text.

5. Keyssar, "Drama and the Dialogic Imagination," 89. Keyssar argues that Bakhtin's resistance to drama stems from his rejection of Aristotle's notion of drama as one action, or unity of plot. Although Keyssar's view is reasonable, there is no specific evidence in Bakhtin's writings to support the claim that he rejected drama on the basis of Aristotle's *Poetics*, with its emphasis on the unity of plot and action. Bakhtin, as this essay shall demonstrate, is concerned with the Hegelian notions of sublation and merging of differing voices that are at times manifest in drama. This is quite different from the Aristotelian notion of unity of plot.

6. Pechey, "On the Borders of Bakhtin," 58.

7. Katerina Clark and Michael Holquist, *Mikhail Bakhtin* (Cambridge: Harvard University Press, 1984), 7. Holquist makes a similar point in his "Introduction: The Architectonics of Answerability," *Art and Answerability: Early Philosophical Essays by M. M. Bakhtin*, Holquist and Vadim Liapunov, eds. (Austin: University of Texas Press, 1990), xxiii.

8. Michael Holquist, *Dialogism: Bakhtin and His World* (London: Routledge, 1990), 24.

9. Gary Saul Morson and Caryl Emerson, *Mikhail Bakhtin: Creation of a Prosaics* (Stanford: Stanford University Press, 1990), 55–56. Morson and Emerson quote from Bakhtin, "Response to a Question from the *Novyi Mir* Editorial Staff," 7.

10. Bakhtin, *Speech Genres and Other Late Essays*, Vern W. McGee, tr. (Austin: University of Texas Press, 1986), 147. For a slightly different translation of the same passage, see Tzvetan Todorov, *Mikhail Bakhtin: The Dialogic Principle*, Wald Godzich, tr. (Minneapolis: University of Minnesota Press, 1995), 104. See also, Morson and Emerson, *Mikhail Bakhtin*, 57.

11. Simon Dentith, *Bakhtinian Thought: An Introductory Reader* (London: Routledge, 1995), 44.

12. M. M. Bakhtin, *Toward a Philosophy of the Act*, Vadim Liapunov and Michael Holquist, eds., V. Liapunov, tr. (Austin: University of Texas Press, 1993), 39.

13. Peter V. Zima, "Bakhtin's Young Hegelian Aesthetics," *Critical Studies* 1.2 (1989): 79, 84.

14. David K. Danow, *The Thoughts of Mikhail Bakhtin: From Word to Culture* (New York: St. Martin's Press, 1991), 60.

15. Bakhtin, "Author and Hero in Aesthetic Activity," *Art and Answerability*, 4.

16. Caryl Emerson, *The First Hundred Years of Mikhail Bakhtin* (Princeton: Princeton University Press, 1997), 219.

17. Michael F. Bernard-Donals, *Mikhail Bakhtin: Between Phenomenology and Marxism* (Cambridge: Cambridge University Press, 1994), 21.

18. Karl Löwith, *From Hegel to Nietzsche: The Revolution in Nineteenth-Century Thought* (David E. Green, tr. (New York: Columbia University Press, 1964), maintains that the writings of the Young Hegelians are "manifestos, programs, and theses, but never anything whole, important in itself. . . . They make immoderate demands with insufficient means, and dilate Hegel's abstract dialectics to a piece of rhetoric." Despite his dismissal of the Young Hegelians, Löwith admits that as "ideologues of growth and movement, they establish themselves upon Hegel's principle of dialectical negativity, and upon the conflict which moves the world" (67).

19. William J. Brazill, *The Young Hegelians* (New Haven: Yale University Press, 1970), 275.

20. Jürgen Habermas, "Left Hegelians, Right Hegelians, and Nietzsche," *The Philosophical Discourse of Modernity*, Frederick G. Lawrence, tr. (Cambridge: MIT Press, 1992), 53.

21. Wolfgang Eßbach, *Die Junghegelianer: Soziologie einer Intellektuellengruppe* (München: Wilhelm Fink, 1988), 20.

22. John Toews, *Hegelianism: The Path toward Dialectical Humanism, 1805–1841* (Cambridge: Cambridge University Press, 1980), 361.

23. G. W. F. Hegel, *Vorlesungen über die Ästhetik III, Werke 15* (Frankfurt/m: Suhrkamp, 1986), 543.

24. Hegel, *The Philosophy of History*, J. Sibree, tr. (New York: Dover Publications, 1956), 71, 72.

25. See, for instance, Georg G. Iggers, *The German Conception of History: The National Tradition of Historical Thought from Herder to the Present* (Middletown, Conn.: Wesleyan University Press, 1968; revised, 1983), 39–40.

26. Broadly speaking, Young Hegelians on the political right were inclined to accept Hegelian reconciliation as symbolic of religious unity.

27. Toews, *Hegelianism*, writes that for the left Hegelians, "a new consciousness of historical change and possibility, of history as something that lay 'before' and was yet to be constructed, rather than as a past that could merely be

comprehended . . . was characteristic of many members of the Hegelian school" (217).

28. Friedrich Hebbel, "Mein Wort über das Drama," *Hebbels Werke* Vol. I (Berlin: Aufbau-Verlag, 1971), 4.

29. Hebbel, "Vorwort zur *Maria Magdalena*," *Hebbels Werke* Vol. I, 98.

30. For a Marxist, "materialist-dialectical" view of Hettner as a "progressive" literary critic, see Hartmut Gruendel, *Der Beitrag Herman Hettners zur Herausbildung der deutschen Literaturgeschichtsschreibung* (Ph. D. Dissertation, Potsdam [DDR], 1984).

31. Hermann Hettner, *Das moderne Drama* (Braunschweig: Bieweg und Sohn, 1852), 109.

32. For a discussion on Bakhtin's relationship to Russian Formalism's materialistic aesthetics, see Gary Saul Morson, "Prosaic Bakhtin: Landmarks, Anti-Intellectualism, and the Russian Countertradition," *Bakhtin in Contexts: Across the Disciplines*, Amy Mandelker, ed. (Evanston: Northwestern University Press, 1995), 55.

33. Bakhtin, *Art and Answerability*, 210. A full comparison of Bakhtin's and Hegel's view of history is beyond the scope of this essay. Suffice it to say, Hegel posited a progressive, positivist approach, whereas Bakhtin favors an architectonic view, incorporating "carnivalistic folklore," or a *"carnival sense of the world"* (*PDP* 107).

34. Julia Kristeva, "Word, Dialogue and Novel," *The Kristeva Reader*, Alice Jardine (et. al.), tr. Toril Moi, ed. (Oxford: Blackwell, 1986), 36.

35. Sven Daelemans and Tullio Maranhão, "Psychoanalytic Dialogue and the Dialogic Principle," *The Interpretation of Dialogue*, Maranhão, ed. (Chicago: University of Chicago Press, 1990), 225.

36. See Bakhtin's discussion on "seeing" in *Toward a Philosophy of the Act*, 62–63.

37. Lisa Eckstrom, "Moral Perception and the Chronotope: The Case of Henry James," *Bakhtin in Contexts: Across the Disciplines*, ed. Amy Mandelker (Evanston, Ill.: Northwestern University Press, 1995), 102.

38. Holquist, *Dialogism*, 151.

39. Holquist, *Dialogism*, 18, 19.

40. For an overview of Bakhtin's relationship to Cohen and the Marburg School, see Holquist, *Dialogism*, 4–5; and Clark and Holquist, *Mikhail Bakhtin*, 58–61.

41. James M. Holquist and Katerina Clark, "The Influence of Kant in the Early Work of M. M. Bakhtin," *Literary Theory and Criticism: Part I: Theory*, Joseph P. Strelka, ed. (Bern: Peter Lang, 1984), 308, 309, passim.

42. In fact, Bakhtin's emphasis is on values, as opposed to Kant's emphasis on knowledge (epistemology).

43. Bernard-Donals, *Mikhail Bakhtin*, 28.

44. Bakhtin, *Art and Answerability*, 1, 2.

45. Todorov, *Mikhail Bakhtin*, 62.

46. Todorov, *Mikhail Bakhtin*, 63.

47. Bakhtin, *Speech Genres*, 126.

48. Rick Bowers, "Bakhtin, Self, and Other: Neohumanism and Communicative Multiplicity," *Canadian Review of Literature* 21.4 (December 1994): 567.

49. Lynne Pearce, *Reading Dialogics* (London: Edward Arnold, 1994), 2.

50. Terry Eagleton, *Literary Theory* (Minnesota: University of Minnesota Press, 1983), 117.

51. Frank Farmer, "Not Theory . . . But a Sense of Theory: The Superaddressee and the Contexts of Eden," *PC Wars: Theory and Politics in the Academy*, Jeffrey Williams, ed. (New York: Routledge, 1995), 209.

52. Devon Boan, "Call-and-Response: Parallel 'Slave Narrative' in August Wilson's *The Piano Lesson*," *African American Review* 32.2 (summer 1998): 263. To be sure, not all of Wilson's plays fit the paradigm of dialectical drama. *Seven Guitars*, for instance, has elements of Bakhtinian dialogics and polyphony. In this play seven characters interact with one another in a related way without unifying or changing each character fundamentally.

53. August Wilson, *The Piano Lesson* (New York: Plume, 1990), 51.

54. Sandra Shannon, *The Dramatic Vision of August Wilson* (Washington, D.C.: Howard University Press, 1995), 147.

55. Kim Pereira, *August Wilson and the African-American Odyssey* (Urbana: University of Illinois Press, 1995), 89.

56. Hans-Georg Gadamer, *Truth and Method*, Joel Weinsheimer and Donald G. Marshall, trs. (New York: Crossroads, 1992), 97.

57. Shange, *for colored girls* (Toronto: Bantam Books, 1977), 44.

58. Daelemans and Maranhão, "Psychoanalytic Dialogue," 226.

59. Ntozake Shange, in Mark Ribowsky, "A Poetess Scores a Hit with [a] Play," *Sepia* 25 (December 1976): 46; quoted in Neal A. Lester, *Ntozake Shange: A Critical Study of the Plays* (New York: Garland, 1995), 26.

60. Emerson, *The First Hundred Years*, 209.

61. Mae Gwendolyn Henderson, "Speaking in Tongues: Dialogics, Dialectics, and the Black Woman Writer's Literary Tradition," *Reading Black, Reading Feminist*, Henry Louis Gates, ed. (New York: 1990), 119. See, also, *Changing Our Own Words: Essays on Criticism, Theory, and Writing by Black Women*, Cheryl A. Wall, ed. (New Brunswick: Rutgers University Press, 1989): 16–37.

62. For an interesting discussion of call and response in relation to Bakhtin, see Dale E. Peterson, "Response and Call: The African American Dialogue with Bakhtin and What It Signifies," *Bakhtin in Contexts*, 89–98.

63. Kristeva, "Word, Dialogue and Novel," 39.

64. V. N. Voloshinov, *Marxism and the Philosophy of Language*, L. Matejka and I. R. Titunik, trs. (Cambridge: Harvard University Press, 1996; 6th printing), 101.

For an informed discussion on the extent of Bakhtin's presence in this text, see Morson and Emerson, "The Disputed Texts," *Mikhail Bakhtin*, 101–19.

65. Mikhail Bakhtin, "Discourse Typology in Prose," *Readings in Russian Poetics: Formalist and Structuralist Views*, L. Matejka and K. Pomorska, eds., R. Balthazar and I. R. Titunik, trs. (Cambridge: MIT Press, 1971), 276.

66. Holquist, *Dialogism*, 152.

67. Morson and Emerson, *Mikhail Bakhtin*, 45.

68. Emerson, *The First Hundred Years*, 36.

69. Holquist, *Dialogism*, 37.

70. Clark and Holquist, *Mikhail Bakhtin*, 78.

71. John Timpane, " 'The Poetry of a Movement': Politics and the Open Form in the Drama of Ntozake Shange," *Studies in American Drama* 4 (1989): 94, 97, 99.

Bakhtin's Ethics and an Iconographic Standard in Crime and Punishment

Jacqueline A. Zubeck

Behold, I send you forth as sheep in the midst of wolves: be ye therefore wise as serpents and harmless as doves

—Mt. 10:16 KJV

Raskolnikov lies on a filthy sofa facing the wall in a stifling Petersburg attic, internalizing the tenets of a utilitarian nihilism—as if these theories might be his very meat and drink. He would make real the principles of these ideologies and accommodate their precepts, swallowing whole the assumptions expressed therein. His character and perspective are such that his ideas are intensified and epitomized as an "abstract cognition", which "seeks to pass itself off as the whole world."[1] Raskolnikov seems keenly suited to illustrate Bakhtin's concerns about theory divorced from practice, or what he refers to as the problem of theoretism. We see Raskolnikov bound to a set of utilitarian principles, which are consistent within a narrow rationalist framework and characterized by an "objective theoretical validity of judgment" (*TPA* 9). But his theoretical standards are removed from actuality and "severed" from his own "answerable consciousness" (*TPA* 29). Raskolnikov obligates himself to a formalistic system and enacts the thinking that is intrinsic to that perspective, imagining that he might do so according to "an essential and fundamental abstraction from the fact" of his "unique being" (*TPA* 9). As such, Raskolnikov illustrates Bakhtin's concerns about a "disembodied theoretical consciousness" (*TPA* 73) which tries to ignore his individual "unique place . . . the answerable . . . concrete center of the concrete manifoldness of the world" (*TPA* 57).

While Raskolnikov's perceptions tend to be blinkered and narrowly focused, the action of the novel as a whole is geared toward a manifestation of the implications of his thinking and renders his theoretical word into flesh. Bakhtin noted that Dostoevsky had an ability to see the "potentialities" of the idea and could "divin[e] how a given idea would develop and function under certain . . . conditions,"[2] a divination that emerges according to his "word made flesh" aesthetics. Thus ideas for Dostoevsky, as for Bakhtin, are never merely theoretical constructs; rather, they reflect the contours of human consciousness and spill out into events.

In this essay I consider Bakhtin's ethical perspective as it is enunciated in "Toward a Philosophy of the Act" and argue that this work is related thematically to "The Idea in Dostoevsky" (from *Problems of Dostoevsky's Art*), in which the critic discusses "the image of the idea," or what he describes as the embodiment of thought in visual characterizations. Finally, I link Bakhtin and Dostoevsky to what I call an "iconographic standard," a perspective which is connected thematically, technically, narratively, and visually to the icon. Because Dostoevsky seeks to make meaning apparent through a "visible" image related to the embodiment of an ideology, it seems reasonable to consider this image in relation to Russian iconography—the wellspring of Russian pictorial and narrative art and the representation of ethical values as well. An iconographic approach pertains to the christological religious sense of both Dostoevsky and Bakhtin, and has bearing on the ideas that both author and critic express in their creative work. Let us historically contextualize the two Bakhtin works in question. Between 1919 and 1921, Bakhtin had worked on a philosophical essay which was published (at long last, in 1986) under the title *K filosofii postupka* (Toward a philosophy of the act).[3] After the completion of this work, Bakhtin turned his attention to Dostoevsky and spent much of his time between 1921 and 1929 working on the Dostoevsky book. "The Idea in Dostoevsky," a chapter from *Problemy tvorchestva Dostoevskogo* (Problems of Dostoevsky's art), was first published in Leningrad in 1929, and expanded and republished in 1963. His notes for further revision emerged in 1971. Caryl Emerson's English translation of the book appeared in 1984 as *Problems of Dostoevsky's Poetics*, and Vadim Liapunov's English translation of the earlier *Act* appeared in 1993. Thus while the publication of these two works seems to locate them in disparate time frames (especially to an English-speaking audience), their composition occurred consecutively and can be linked, I will argue, conceptually.

The historical period in which the two works were written also seems significant. The 1920s heralded the beginning of the long Soviet night. During this time, Bakhtin experienced firsthand the evolution of Marxism-Leninism. He witnessed the consequences of a theory run rampant, and saw actual practice made negligible in the primacy of a paradigm. One could not, of course, directly address the dangerous issue of political theory and actual practice during this period. But "Three Fragments from the 1929 Edition," which did not appear in the 1963 version, speaks to the terrifying concerns that Bakhtin had during the composition of these works and may signify his anticipation of official censorship of both topic and approach. In the foreword to the book, Bakhtin noted that he "had to exclude all historical problems," although "this approach to the material" cannot be considered "methodologically correct or normal"—in relation to socialist realism and its deterministic historical perspective. He makes a point of linking "every literary work" to "social evaluations" and seems eager to justify his own work in regard to an author whose art had managed to "outliv[e]" his suspect "philosophical and sociopolitical ideology" (*PDP* 276). Reading between the lines (a characteristic practice of the time) suggests that Bakhtin had concerns about the primacy of theory in Soviet Russia and the barbaric practices used to instill a monologic ideology into human consciousness and behavior. He had to mask these life-threatening matters with rhetoric that would appease Soviet censors, however, and emphasized, for example, Dostoevsky's "revolutionary innovation" in fiction.

We might also consider the thematic link between the two works. Some of the concerns in the Dostoevsky book about the *incarnation* of an idea resonate with the central problem of "Toward a Philosophy of the Act." In the latter, Bakhtin discusses the ethical problems, which accrue to the individual who embraces a theory that is consistent within a logical framework, but which does not take into account human consciousness and the particularity of context. Bakhtin thought in terms of the *word made flesh*, and in a typical first-person formulation insisted that "[e]very thought of mine, along with its content, is an act or deed that I perform— my own individually answerable act or deed [*postupok*]" (*TPA* 3). This statement, found in the first pages of *Act*, informs the work as a whole. Bakhtin's "ethics of incarnation," if we may call it that, serves as a way to confront the dichotomy between theory and practice—by considering theory *as* practice. Theory as practice implies a weighted, active, individual acknowledgment of one's ideas in a way that "concentrates, correlates, and resolves within a unitary and unique and . . . *final context* both the sense and the fact, the universal and the individual, the real and the ideal" (*TPA* 28).

"The Idea in Dostoevsky" relates to this notion of a unitary and unique embodiment of thought as action. The "image of the idea"[4] suggests a literary visualization of theory in relation to the materiality of the world. It connotes that the idea has a palpability about it, a specificity which is played out in the world at large. Bakhtin suggests that Dostoevsky makes an idea tangible by personifying it—by making it an intrinsic part of a personality. Dostoevsky's hero is "inseparably linked with the image of an idea" so that the idea reaches into "the deepest recesses of his personality" ("Idea" 87). Raskolnikov's character illustrates this idea-driven personality—a character *particularly suited* to a self-lacerating adherence to formal structure. He experiences ideology at the level of *strast'*—with a passion that is related to compulsion, crucifixion, and love. But it is in the physical presentation and external manifestation of an inner intellectual and moral phenomenon that "[w]e *see* the hero in the idea and through the idea, and we *see* the idea in him and through him" ("Idea" 87). This kind of visual evocation is implied when Dostoevsky writes (in regard to another work): "the *dominating idea* of the Life must be visible . . . although *the entire dominating idea will not be explained in words. . . .*"[5] The dominating idea is the psychological stuff of the character himself, and suggests a unified context, an integration between ideology and psychology. Thus Dostoevsky "tried to perceive and formulate each thought in such a way that a whole person was expressed and began to sound in it." The "idea" involved "an entire spiritual orientation" which "emerged not [as] a system," but as "a concrete event" ("Idea" 93).

The enactment or contextualization of an idea was especially important to Dostoevsky in relation to *Crime and Punishment,* in which the author's artistic goal was, among other things, to make manifest the implications of radical theory. Joseph Frank notes that Dostoevsky had a "close personal contact . . . with a wide and diversified range of Russian social-cultural opinion. Indeed, he could see all its nuances *embodied in the flesh* as he spoke to the youthful members of the younger generation who swarmed into the editorial offices of his journal."[6] In other words, Dostoevsky saw various contemporary theories in terms of the particular individuals who held those ideas. But the author considered many of these philosophies to be simplistic in tone and naïve in conception. He was disturbed by the "strange, 'unfinished'" quality of the day's rhetoric and mourned an impoverished perspective, which, tragically, had little effect on the *sincerity* of the believers (*The Stir of Liberation* 42). Dostoevsky noted, for example, that the tremendous influence of nihilism in Russia came "in the name of honor, truth, and genuine usefulness." He empathized with this impulse and saw in it, it would seem, his own youthful goals and aspirations. Twenty years later, he also comprehended the "calamitous results" of naïvely conceived perspectives, while feeling "sorrow and pity for all the innocents who are being misled by such doctrines."[7] In *Crime and Punishment,* he creates a protagonist, a "man of the idea" ("Idea" 85), who embraces completely the tenets of radical thought, and, in the long process of the novel, comes to understand the ruinous consequences of his abstract conceptions—according to the weight of his own participation.

It is noteworthy that Bakhtin also considers the human personality as "unfinalized and inexhaustible" so that, in a sense, the "inexhaustible" nature of human identity speaks of the complexity of the idea and its various and variable consequences in the world. Bakhtin writes: "The idea is by nature dialogic." It "begins to live . . . to take shape, to develop . . . only when it enters into genuine dialogic relationships with other ideas, with the ideas of *others*" ("Idea" 86, 88). In Dostoevsky's novels, the meaning of an ideology is enacted or realized in relation to other consciousnesses within unique contexts in which "the idea is posed in terms beyond affirmation and repudiation, [and] at the same time [is] not reduced to simple psychical experience" ("Idea" 80). In *Crime and Punishment,* the embodied event, implied in ideological form, makes itself felt in such a way that the protagonist comes to acknowledge his "own participation in unitary Being-as-event," a "fact [which] cannot be adequately expressed in theoretical terms, but can only be . . . participatively experienced" (*TPA* 40). In the novel, Dostoevsky takes an ideology related to "utility," gives it to a personality that devours the idea and makes it part of his very being, and places him in the midst of other consciousnesses within specific events. It is among these characters, within the unique texture of *their* particular contexts, that the significance of the idea is disclosed. All the characters, acting within the various associations of the novel, actualize the psychological, theoretical, and interactive potential of an ideology, associations which fatten into particular occurrences. Thus it is in the various manifestations of an "inexhaustible" human nature—in relation to other inexhaustible natures—in which the "image of the fully valid idea" emerges ("Idea" 86). In this way, the idea becomes "a live event, a dialogic meeting between two or several consciousnesses." And within this interactive field, ideas yield up their "various facts, nuances, [and] possibilities" ("Idea" 88). Dostoevsky manifests this individualized, yet dialogic quality of the idea in his signature scenes in which a group of characters, who embody "integral life positions," participate in a particular scene, "under conditions of living contact with another and alien thought . . . thought[s] embodied in someone else's voice" ("Idea" 88).

Raskolnikov, of course, strives to avoid these dialogic interactions and to hold the idea close to his chest, as if its workings affect him and him alone. His narcissistic deliberations regarding his own Napoleonic distinction and the utilitarian evaluations in regard to the pawnbroker provide little room for the consideration of the actual implications of his ideas, to be made incarnate with terrible effect in the world. Raskolnikov represses consideration of the consequences of thought and the particular contexts in which his philosophy is to be enacted. Instead, he struggles to maintain allegiance to his own theoretical formulations—and necessarily discards disorderly human particularity. Striving to confine himself to the "chief point,"[8] Raskolnikov bridles an acknowledgment of the physical reality of the murder and takes a disembodied perspective, which renders physical particularity and prosaic detail inconsequential. He wraps his ideas, like the decoy pledge, "carefully and daintily in clean, white paper," but "never for a single instant all that time could [he] believe in the carrying out of his plans" (*CP* 62). Fulfillment of the act, "the actual—individual and historical—self-activity of the performed act" (*TPA* 26) fades away in the light of a singular demonstration of his "will and reasoning power" (*CP* 64). But this "will-as-deed produces the law to which it submits," and as such, "describes a circle," that which "shuts itself in" from other human consciousnesses according to a "theoretism" that Bakhtin describes as "fatal" (*TPA* 27). Raskolnikov's decision is morally catastrophic because it neglects "an actual acknowledgment of one's own participation in unitary Being-as-event," and throws Raskolnikov, instead, into "irresponsible self-surrender" to his own Napoleonic pronouncements and theoretical formulations (*TPA* 27, 49). Thus he proceeds according to an "abstraction" from the self, as Bakhtin suggests, that is, from a sense of his own inescapable presentness within particular human interactions. He "doggedly, slavishly [seeks] arguments in all directions" to rationalize the murder within his Napoleonic framework, "as though someone were forcing and drawing him to it" (*CP* 63).

Robert Louis Jackson and Gary Saul Morson both discuss Raskolnikov's moral abdication in ways that are relevant to Bakhtin's perspective. Jackson notes that "Raskolnikov will never decide to commit the crime. He will never consciously, actively, and with his whole moral being choose to kill—or, the reverse, choose not to kill. . . . And yet he will kill! He will lose his freedom . . . and be pulled into crime and murder—so it will seem to him—by some 'unnatural power.'"[9] Caught up in the nihilist romance of Napoleon and the abstract numbers of "utility," Raskolnikov adopts an ideology whose workings are such that they justify even murder. Yet this weighted, bloody act is not something that the protagonist actively considers. His musings are not considered part of a "necessary moment in the composition of the performed act" and are kept strangely remote from the actual commission of the deed. As Morson argues, Raskolnikov "does not settle details *in order to* remain in uncertainty, *in order to* stay in the territory between deciding to act and deciding not to act."[10] Raskolnikov dreams of nihilistic power and utilitarian virtue, but never actually settles on the means for achieving these ends. (This is, in part, why he is fascinated by coincidence: when he overhears the conversation between the young officer and his friend proposing the murder of the pawnbroker, he feels that his role is justified and inevitable.) Raskolnikov "at last arrives at a moment when not renouncing the action necessitates doing it, *though without a decision to do so*" (emphasis added). It is as if the murders occur entropically, eked out in the "shrinking space between resolution and renunciation," as Raskolnikov "continues to do the sheer minimum necessary to keep the dream alive." Nevertheless, the "minimum is enough to bring [Raskolnikov] to the murder scene, axe in hand" (*Narrative and Freedom* 226).

Raskolnikov has adopted an alibi and falls into an "irresponsible self-surrender to being" in his blind adherence to a theory "governed by its own immanent laws" (*TPA* 7, 49). But he suppresses an "attitude of consciousness" which considers the theoretical along with the practical aspects of its exploration, the repercussions implied in the theory itself (*TPA* 24). Raskolnikov tries to divorce theory from practice even as he puts into effect the bloodiest kind of act in relation to his ideas, as if the purity of the concept releases him from the corruption of the deed. But in this division, he also abdicates "the uniqueness of [his] participation in Being" (*TPA* 41), a participation which Bakhtin characterizes as "answerability."

"Answerability" refers to a link between "the sense and the fact," "the real and the ideal." It involves "a thoughtful response to particular events," and has the sense of a "performed act [which] constitutes a going out *once and for all* from within possibility as such into *what is once-occurrent*" (*TPA* 28–29). In other words, answerability involves a willingness to see one's ideas (theoretical "possibility") in terms of a particular ("once-occurrent") event. Bakhtin writes that "the evaluation of a thought as an individual act . . . takes into account and includes within itself . . . the theoretical validity of a thought *qua* judgment" which must be considered in terms of a "necessary moment in the composition of the performed act" (*TPA* 3–4). In other words, one's theories occur with an intellectual substance and pith relating to how one spends the minutes of one's life. To disregard this weight is to be both dangerously naïve and morally remiss; to acknowledge responsibility for one's ideas is to be discerning and morally answerable. Answerability also implies an adoption of what Bakhtin calls "my non-alibi in Being" (*TPA* 40), which he characterizes as an "attitude of consciousness" (*TPA* 24) that affirms and acknowledges "the uniqueness of my participation in Being" (*TPA* 41). Answerability implies an active position, not an "irresponsible self-surrender to being" (*TPA* 49) nor a blind adherence to a theory "governed by its own laws" (*TPA* 7). The "non-alibi in Being" suggests moral struggle in relation to the daily and ongoing social events and interactions—that specific time and space in which moral responsibility has its place, and where "I assume answerability for my own uniqueness" (*TPA* 42). I must sign my name, Bakhtin says, to the events of daily interaction. This signing is related to "authorship" as well. One authors one's deeds as one would author one's books, the signing implying an acknowledgment of one's answerable participation.

Raskolnikov offers an "alibi in Being" when, for example, he comes upon the drunken young girl stalked by a well-dressed dandy. He wants to intercede on her behalf, but he quickly belittles this impulse and abandons the girl. Let them "devour each other," he decides; after all, a certain "percentage" will always be sacrificed (*CP* 45). In this case, Raskolnikov retreats into the abstract formulas of utilitarianism, a theory whose "autonomy" seems to be "justified and inviolable" (*TPA* 7), or "scientific" and backed by numerical "evidence." Raskolnikov declines to participate morally and, in regard to this unrepeatable event, will not "assume answerability for [his] own uniqueness" (*TPA* 42). He will not, as Bakhtin says, sign his name to that specific incident or be answerable for his involvement in it. Instead, he retreats into formulas: "once you've said 'percentage,' there's nothing more to worry about." Percentages "are so scientific, so consolatory" (*CP* 45).

In this interaction, Raskolnikov considers the young girl as an abstract entity. But this abstraction serves to effect an absenting of himself as well. He tells the bewildered policeman not to interfere with the girl and her pursuer and "long[s] to forget himself altogether, to forget everything" (*CP* 45). He does not want to be connected to this particular interaction or even be conscious of it, and "removes himself" by referring to his well-defined theoretical formula, which, as Bakhtin notes, "makes me myself useless" (*TPA* 9). Raskolnikov illustrates the neglect and negation of what Bakhtin calls "my own unique place in Being," the "actual center from which my act or deed can issue" (*TPA* 43). Thus he retreats from a sense of answerability, offers up a utilitarian "alibi," and funnels the girl into an element of an equation, into "an essential and fundamental abstraction from the fact of [her] unique Being . . .'as if [she] did not exist'" (*TPA* 9). According to the strict dictates of his theory, her individuality, as is his, is beside the point. Porfiry Petrovich, the police investigator who pursues Raskolnikov, specifically deals with formal configurations in relation to actual practice. He reminds Raskolnikov that "the general case . . . calculated and laid down in books, does not exist at all, for the reason [that] every case, every crime . . . as soon as it actually occurs, at once becomes a thoroughly special case" (CP 294). Raskolnikov's "thoroughly special case" emerges despite its genesis according to a generalized, "universally valid" law, a law which cannot, however, accommodate the potential of a "unique and concrete, never to be repeated actuality" (TPA 73). Raskolnikov, putting his stock into utilitarian guidelines, proceeds according to "the detached content of the cognitional act . . . governed by its own immanent laws" (TPA 7).

Act translator Vadim Liapunov suggests that the problem with "universally valid" laws, especially those which espouse no specifically ethical norms, is that they demand a sense of obligation to the abstract paradigm or perspective itself (TPA 84). This commitment illustrates what Bakhtin called a "law of conformity to the law" (TPA 27). But the sense of obligation to an abstract paradigm can become, in Liapunov's words, "an inexhaustible source of moral nihilism"—in which the destruction of traditional moral ideas or standards of behavior becomes the "moral" act (TPA 84). [11] In Raskolnikov's case, the faithfulness to a utilitarian paradigm exists almost as a challenge: to put into effect its precepts according to a strict letter-of-the-law conformity, even if it means the annihilation of all other moral standards. This perspective is analogous to that of Nikolai Pisarev, when he suggested that nihilists should "[s]trike right and left; what resists the blow is worth keeping, what flies to pieces is rubbish anyway" (quoted in MY 70). (This idea is paraphrased by Raskolnikov in the confession scene in which he tries to explain to Sonia why he committed the murders [CP 286–87].)

At this point I want to consider the dynamic which links Raskolnikov's nihilism to his utilitarianism, two concepts which may seem antithetical at first. Nihilism, with its distrust and rejection of all traditional moral teachings or perspectives, places a great deal of emphasis on the "extraordinary man" who has an ability to speak a "new word," as Raskolnikov says, and who is not constrained by "prejudice" or preexisting norms. The protagonist explains to Porfiry Petrovich that "ordinary people are conservative in temperament and law abiding. They live under control and love to be controlled." But the extraordinary man sees morality as a matter of personal discretion. He requires no consideration of other persons or the prosaic matters which interfere with his agenda. Rare individuals, like "Lycurgus, Solon, Mahomet, Napoleon . . . were all without exception criminals," says Raskolnikov, and "transgressed the ancient [law]" (CP 226). But it is their transgression which makes them great and their "greatness" which makes transgression a "moral act." Raskolnikov, similarly, constructs himself as paradigm and precedent and proceeds as if all individuals or ideas are subordinated to the measure of his self-regarded genius.

The "extraordinary" man, by definition an individual with an exaggerated sense of self and considered the foundation and yardstick of morality, has an odd kind of moral authority. Raskolnikov argues that if he "is forced for the sake of his idea to step over a corpse or wade through blood, he can . . . find within himself, *in his conscience,* a sanction for wading through blood" (*CP* 227). It is Razumikhin who understands the implications of Raskolnikov's idea (perhaps with Dostoevsky's sense of a higher "reality"). [12] He notes that conscience-sanctioned murder is "more terrible than the official, legal sanction" because crime is then validated as a *principle.*

In seeking to make real in himself the ideal of the extraordinary man, Raskolnikov works with a single-mindedness akin to madness. The intense focus necessary for the enactment of his goal is attractive to Raskolnikov and complements his own personal characteristics, drawn as he is to isolation and, like the nihilist hero Bazarov, immensely conceited. He has systematically cut his social ties and retires to a cramped and filthy attic room, one more expression of his antisocial outlook. Here he cooks himself into a fevered frenzy so that he might demonstrate his "greatness." Raskolnikov "had gotten completely away from everyone, like a tortoise in its shell" and "was in the condition that overtakes some monomaniacs entirely concentrated upon one thing" (*CP* 25). Moreover, he jealously guards the isolation that produces his concentrated dream, the blinkered perception which blinds him to actual contexts and the prosaic actuality of events in the world. Again, Porfiry Petrovich provides the appropriate analysis of Raskolnikov's condition: "You lead such a solitary life that you know nothing of matters that concern you directly" (*CP* 225).

Raskolnikov, of course, refers to the rhetoric of utilitarianism, but this is a philosophy stripped down to bare essentials and simplistic in nature. Its very lack of complexity allows for attention to be paid to what really counts for Raskolnikov—himself. Like Emmerich in Don DeLillo's *The Names,* he is "self-taught, self-willed," but his theoretical guidelines form "endless material for speculation and self-knowledge." [13] This narcissistic emphasis on self is justified and supported by a rhetoric which stresses the abstract nature of the other (as a percentage or an expendable entity paving the way for a "better" future). Particularity, signaled by the prosaic, the earthy, and the contingent, fades away in the glare of the central concept. Thus even as he gathers the materials to commit the murder and descends the steps to the kitchen to pick up the axe, "he was thinking of the chief point, and put off trifling details" (*CP* 63). The "trifling details" are, Bakhtin might say, precisely the issue. Where Bakhtin would "linger intently" over the "valued manifoldness of Being as human" (*TPA* 64), Raskolnikov plays the role of the "superior man" and collapses other individuals into material made over in the service of his "chief point."

Both concepts that concern Raskolnikov—the notion of the exceptional man and utilitarianism—imply the necessity of an adherence or commitment to the law or standard—"for the sake of the law," as Bakhtin says. These ethical concepts are categorical in their absence of attention to circumstance or context, while having reference only to their own circumscribed form. They imply a "principle of abstract ought or obligation" in reference to their own form and posit "the good" in terms of the principle itself, but this hypothesis has nothing to do with behavior or a consideration of what one "ought" to do in relation to another person. And as Liapunov notes, "the principle of abstract ought or obligation has demonstrated a frightening perversity to conceive the "ought as the . . . *absence* of any ought." In other words, abstract perspectives which refer only to themselves can all too easily degenerate into the destruction of traditional moral behavior as the "proof" that the idea governs everything. Thus these perspectives prove to be "an inexhaustible source of moral nihilism" (*TPA* 84). It is important to note, of course, that Raskolnikov's sense of superiority and concomitant loathing for other people is only a part of his complex character. Frank argues that Raskolnikov's nihilism also "run[s] counter to the instinctive promptings of his moral-emotive sensibility" (*MY* 107), a sensibility which relates, I would argue, to his Orthodox Christian background. This perspective makes itself apparent, for example, after Marmeladov is killed and Raskolnikov gives all of his money to his widow to pay for the funeral. Shortly thereafter, little Polenka clasps him about the neck and hugs him warmly; a tender feeling envelops Raskolnikov and moves him toward an uncharacteristic humility. He asks the child to pray for "thy servant Rodion," and after this brief interlude he feels that he "ha[s] not yet died with that old woman! The Kingdom of Heaven to her." In effect, he says a brief prayer for the repose of her soul and for himself.

Raskolnikov's very name implies a split within the character: *raskol* means "dissidence" or "schism." This dichotomy appears throughout the novel, in the scene with the drunken girl previously mentioned, and in the dream of the beaten mare as well. In the latter, Raskolnikov as a child sees the small, well-loved cemetery church in the distance. He remembers it tenderly for its "frameless icons" and green cupola. But the child moves on in the dream, away from the church, and comes to watch helplessly as the little mare is brutally beaten to death by her drunken master. Here we witness the mindless and obsessive enactment of the implications of another kind of utilitarian perspective. (Is the mare useful?) The point here is that Raskolnikov and the drunken peasant in the dream each behave in an "almost wholly mechanica[l]" fashion, "as if a piece of his clothing had been caught in the cogs of a machine and he were dragged into it."[14] It is as if Raskolnikov and the peasant cast themselves into the abyss of their intoxication, ideological or otherwise, an inebriation so complete that we might say it "describes a circle, shuts itself in, and exclude[s] the actual." This suggests a nihilistic intoxication, each man drunk with the power to destroy. And yet each one acts without the "actualization of a *decision*," as Bakhtin says (*TPA* 26, 7).

The novel, however, provides a ballast against the "weightlessness" of Raskolnikov's ideas. As a utilitarian nihilist, Raskolnikov is conceptually unable or unwilling to accommodate the heavy reality of human flesh and human context. He cannot imagine the form his ideas will eventually take because individual "form" itself is denigrated by the very notion of utilitarian percentages or nihilistic destruction. Morson notes that "[a]t the murder scene, [Raskolnikov] is 'almost unconscious of his body'" (*Narrative and Freedom* 227). And yet, the novel makes manifest the "image" of the protagonist's "idea"—his word represented in the bloody corpses of his victims. This grotesque incarnation of Raskolnikov's ideology in the novel occurs, I will argue, in relation to the Eastern Christian cultural-religious tradition implied in the text, a tradition which stresses the Incarnation of Jesus Christ and the "Word made flesh." Raskolnikov's ideology emerges in relation to other characters. But we might say that it also occurs as a conscious reaction to Christian thought and posits its diametrical opposition to the principles implied in Eastern Christianity and expressed visually in the icon.

In order to discuss these ideals, let us first consider a brief history of iconography. Icons, consisting of images of Christ and his disciples, various saints, and particular religious events, appeared from the earliest days of the Christian religion. By the fourth century, theologians and Christian thinkers such as John Chrysostom, Basil the Great, Gregory the Theologian, and Gregory of Nyssa refer "to images as to a normal and generally accepted institution of the Church."[15] Despite Jewish proscriptions against images, worries of church leaders regarding idolatry, and a bitter iconoclastic period, iconography took "its natural place in Church practice" (*Icons* 27). The logic and justification of iconography is related, I want to stress, to the Eastern Orthodox emphasis on the Incarnation of Jesus Christ, who was considered to be "the express image of (the Father's) person" (John 1:18, Heb. 1:3). This was the Son who was anticipated by the prophets and who embodied the ideals and teachings of the Father—*His* word made flesh. This Incarnation was seen as the fulfillment of a long Hebrew prophetic tradition. Christian theologians and thinkers thus considered it legitimate to move "from the symbols of the Old Testament . . . to a representation of what they symbolized, to the uncovering of their direct meaning." This "direct meaning" relates to a figure who was "accessible to sensory perception, representation, and description" (*Icons* 28). The materiality of the incarnate Christ, represented in the material form of the icon, is the message—because a keen sense of Christ's embodiment "lies at the foundation" of Orthodox "pictorial art" (*Icons* 31). As Ouspensky affirms, "the image not only does not contradict the essence of Christianity, but, being its basic truth, is inalienably connected with it" (*Icons* 28).

In this paper I connect the icon to what might be called a prosaic ethic, which we can think about in terms of Orthodox values related to the Incarnation. Prosaic ethics are related to both humility (*God* made man) and the possibility of an ennobled human reality (God made *man*). The icon speaks of the dignity and value of the human form and the best possibilities inherent therein. Its underlying theme of incarnation implies not only the embodiment of an ideal, but the possibility that the viewer might also embody a similar ideal. Iconography, using a sophisticated artistic technique, that of inverse perspective, seems to invite the viewer into the plane of the icon. Inverse perspective does not create depth and distance as does realistic perspective, but implies the inclusion of the viewer within the scene itself. Let us consider, for example, Andrei Rublev's depiction of the Holy Trinity, in which the three angels sit at a table facing the viewer. One has the impression that one might join them there and sit in their midst. This is precisely the point. The perspective of the icon suggests an invitation into the icon because it creates visually a liminal realm in which the viewer is given a place—as if the incarnation of an ideal might be the province of the individual viewer—as well as the province of Christ.

The icon's appeal to the individual viewer is related to the emphasis on individual identity in Eastern Christian art. Often described as "static," the depictions on icons actually attest to the physical image of the person. For nearly two thousand years, for example, John the Baptist has been depicted with a certain cowlick curl in his hair, peculiar to a man who lived in the desert and ate locusts. But this small feature is important because it identifies *this* particular man and his unique appearance in the world. Iconographic form pays attention to personality and detail. As Ouspensky notes, "[t]he Church does not reject particularities connected with human nature or with time and place . . . but sanctifies their content" [*Icons* 30]. Moreover, the concern with particular identity and the physical characteristics of a man is one indication of the valorization of the material body that is part of the Eastern Christian tradition. Orthodoxy proffers no Manichean dichotomy between flesh and spirit and no concentration on "original sin" as a fundamental basis of human existence. A much different approach to physical reality is implied, for example, in Orthodox liturgical services, which appeal to the eye and the ear, the nose and the palate, and use color, choreography, and the weighted distinctions of fasting and feast to underscore the ineluctible intersection of body and soul.

A prosaic ethic contrasts markedly, of course, with the denigration of the quotidian implied in "extraordinary man" scenarios or in Raskolnikov's conception of human beings as dissolute by definition and "truly defective by nature" ("Philosophical Pro and Contra in Part One of *Crime and Punishment*" 192). When he meets Marmeladov and hears about Sonia, Raskolnikov growls "man grows used to everything, the scoundrel!" And yet this divided character also asks: "What if I am wrong? What if man is not really a scoundrel, man in general . . . then all the rest is prejudice, simply artificial terror and there are no barriers and it's all as it should be" (*CP* 24). If man is not a scoundrel . . . then there are no barriers. First, the condition which affects "man in general" relates to a universal condition, one marked, in the nihilist mind, by natural law and the perimeters imposed by a human "species." If one cannot escape the boundaries of a deterministic science, then in order to be exceptional ("not a scoundrel"), one must acknowledge strictly materialist conditions and at the same time, epitomize the possibilities of the species. To do so, one must accept the premise of a deterministic law and put into practice—without fear or trembling—the implications of that understanding, which includes the leveling of all moral foundations or meaningful standards. Ethical standards are merely conventional in the face of materialist foundations and serve only to demonstrate "prejudice" and "artificial terror," as Raskolnikov says. But the epitome of the species—the exceptional man—enacts a laying waste of standards and acts according to a nihilistically conceived environment, taking at face value the materialist concepts which level ethics, leaving the ground free for the utterance of the "new word," the thing that "men most fear."

Raskolnikov's point of view, we might say, occurs according to an "exclusive" perspective, one which considers the value of "extraordinary" characters and relegates the "ordinary" to the ranks of the negligible and inconsequential. Putting himself into the extraordinary category, Raskolnikov develops an "exclusive" perspective, framed in terms of his ego, which becomes the "I" (or "eye") that sees outward into an immense world. He is the "one-eyed motionless person who is clearly detached from what he sees. [Realistic perspective] makes a god of the spectator, who becomes the person *on whom the world converges*, the Unmoved Onlooker."[16] We can think about Hughes's description in relation to Raskolnikov's overwhelming emphasis on self, as if we might imagine him at the "vanishing point" in a diagram which traces the point of view of realistic drawing on which all objects converge.

An iconographic point of view, created through inverse perspective, creates not depth and distance, but a sense of inclusion within the plane of the image, as mentioned earlier in the discussion in regard to Rublev's *Holy Trinity*. Continuing in this vein, we can consider the "inclusiveness" of iconographic art as a contiguous threshold created by inverse perspective. Consider the icons depicting the Nativity of Christ. There the infant Christ is situated at the very center of the icon (implying his semantic dominance in the image). Yet He is clearly a being of the earth, lying within a cave that houses an ox and ass. The inclusion of these animals relates to the prophet Isaiah's words "the ox and the ass know their master's crib" and implies the presence of the Old Testament prophecy within the depicted scene, linking two historical periods. Peripheral figures surround the infant but retain their own identities, the particularities of their individual characters working to broaden the story of the child and providing a hermeneutic direction in which to regard the central figure. Thus we see Mary, the Mother of Christ, pictured closest to her son, the three kings offering their gifts of frankincense, gold, and myrrh, indicative of his priesthood, kingship, and death, and the angels rejoicing in the heavens. The interaction implied here suggests a unity or unified realm between earth and heaven, birth and death, old and new. Sometimes we see the child being bathed, which again stresses the earthly quality of the heavenly king. We might also consider the various individuals depicted in relation to their own threshold condition, on the edge of two realities. Humble shepherds behold an angelic choir and the kings are guided by a star. Perhaps most interesting is the figure of Joseph, the "just man" who had been plagued by doubt from the time of the Annunciation, when he was tempted to "put away" his pregnant betrothed "quietly." Here he sits on the very edge of the frameless icon, replicating the viewer's own misgivings about the virgin birth and the incarnation of God. But here, too, his connection to the viewer from within the plane of the icon itself implies another kind of threshold interaction and speaks of the importance of the viewer and his inclusion in the plane of the iconographic space.

Let us compare inverse perspective to its conceptual opposite, realistic perspective. Realistic perspective holds the viewer at arm's length and makes "the presentation . . . a view, a spectacle, an object of our gaze."[17] Inverse perspective, on the other hand, "presupposes an internal position of the artist" who "may be conceived of as being located *in the depths of the picture*" itself. From this perspective, "the artist is not isolated from the world he represents, but places himself in the position of an observer involved in it."[18] This internally located observer/artist depicts "not the object itself," but "the space surrounding this object (the world in which it is located)." Uspensky goes on to describes the multiple outlooks that this perspective generates, what he calls a "multilateral visual embrace" or "summation" of various internal points of view. This visual embrace does not create a single, fixed point of view, but encourages the eye to move around the image, as if it took up the various vantage points of the persons depicted within. But this summation suggests that "the entire picture as a whole becomes a SIGN of the reality represented, and its individual fragments are correlated to their *denotata* not directly, but through the relation of both to the whole" (Uspensky 34, 38). In other words, the icon presupposes the semantic importance of all the elements in the image so that their detachment (the detailed view) does not work for the icon, in contrast to realistic painting, in which "a detail can be removed" and still retain its "relation to the real world." People or items in realistic works can be isolated within the picture and continue to be meaningful in that isolation, whereas in the icon, where all the figures are postured around a semantic center, details appear somewhat distorted when taken out of context. Here artistic technique complements philosophical position as the icon constructs a world in which each of the persons inhabiting the iconographic scene lives a gestalt greater than the self. Thus iconography emphasizes the "relative correlation" of the human elements and "not so much in the concrete representation itself" (Uspensky 34, 35). What is important here is the sense of inclusion, the meaningful participation, of all those depicted within the embodied ideal of the icon.

We may note here that the sense of the inclusive realm incorporated into the iconographic approach to art is intimately related to Orthodox Christian ritual. There is constant participatory activity in the body of the church. (This is why traditional churches have no fixed seating in the center of the church.) During the services, people move throughout the space of the temple. They greet one another, venerate the icons, and light candles. And in the very center of the church, they are baptized, married, and mourned. Charles Lock considers the physically participatory nature of Orthodox worship and, in so doing, discusses the difference between depth-creating realistic perspective and an inclusive iconographic point of view. He writes:

> Perspective dissociates the image from the material by which it is consti-
> tuted. What is within the frame is untouchable—and the frame is introduced
> as a condition of perspective (as the proscenium arch becomes a condition
> of theatre, and the isolation of the object of inquiry a condition of Baconian
> scientific method): the frame is that through which the subject of modernity
> is constituted, by a radical separation from the object of modernity—the
> object of modern knowledge. The optical becomes supreme, and the senses
> are valued insofar as they operate over distances. The immaterialization
> of the image, its disembodiment, leads to a disembodiment of the subject,
> whose body is reduced to being a pedestal for the eyes, and the ears. ("Iconic
> Space and the Materiality of the Sign" 2)

Here Lock lays out the modern, panoptic object of inquiry implied in realistic perspective. The distance suggested by realism isolates the viewer and disembodies him—because only the eyes are working. One can only *see* in the distance. There is no sense of being enveloped by the inverse perspective of the icon or by the choreography of the liturgical service. Counterintuitively, realistic perspective brings about "[t]he immaterialization of the image, its disembodiment" because, in a sense, one has no immediate connection to the milieu. There seems to be no physical body involved and therefore "the disembodiment of the subject is implied." And, as he says, this disembodiment "marks the end of ritual." Lock defines "ritual" thus: "a field of representation which includes the subject as a human body and which excludes the spectatorship of the subject. . . . In considering ritual we should speak of participation and of embodiment—that is, the valorization of the body as both ground and figure of semiotic value" ("Iconic Space and the Materiality of the Sign" 2).

Lock's definition implies the dignity of the human form and its expressive participation in liturgical services, again placing semiotic value on every individual. In a sense, the reality of the incarnation is evoked by ritualistic (or social) interaction within the church, calling upon the specificity of the flesh, considered noble within this inclusive sphere and appealed to by music, color, choreography, and scent.

That the liminality of the icon and the inclusionary, participatory realm created by iconographic technique, as well as the semantic importance of all the "participants," may be considered in relation to Bakhtin's ethics. Bakhtin considers "my actual participation in time and space from my unique place in Being" as the standpoint or foundation from which one might behave answerably (TPA 59). He affirms our particular situatedness in the world, and notes that this positioning implies all kinds of contiguous relations and threshold interactions. We cannot cut ourselves off from this liminal condition with respect to other individuals, for they, too, must be incorporated or considered within the whole picture. Thus he considers ethics not as a system or a "systematic inventory of values" or a matter of pure concepts, but a responsibility which occurs vis-à-vis "the actual, concrete architectonic of value-governed experiencing of the world . . . with that actual, concrete center (both spatial and temporal) from which valuations, assertions, and deeds come forth" (TPA 61). He speaks of the individual consciousness embodied, weighted and inescapably centered in the world, and yet conceived to be on a threshold with other embodied consciousnesses. This liminality is what makes all the factors pertinent, both human and contextual, and which is "iconographic" in its inclusivity, attentive to the uniqueness of both the individual and the circumstance. It is a perspective which suggests "a unitary and unique . . . context" which pays attention to "the sense and the fact, the universal and the individual, the real and the ideal" (TPA 28, 29).

The sense of a physical literalness within a participatory realm corresponds also to the ethical sense of Dostoevsky and Bakhtin, in their search for a unity between theory and practice. Dostoevsky's famous preference to remain with Christ, even if He is a "mistake," is a predilection which Bakhtin interprets in terms of the author's skepticism about "truth in the theoretical sense of the word . . . truth as formula, truth as proposition" ("Idea" 98). Dostoevsky wanted his truth incarnate, weighted and attentive to the prosaic necessities of life in the world. And yet, he also thought it essential to consider Christ as "the ideal image," but incarnate and related to practical activity in the world. "How would Christ have acted?" seems to be Dostoevsky's approach to ethical evaluation and ethical action ("Idea" 98). This is a prosaic approach to ethics, sensitive to the nuance of individual context—but firmly planted before an ideal that has also been embodied in the flesh.

Dostoevsky's ethical approach suggests an active and ongoing evaluation of thought and action with regard to the ideal of Jesus Christ, whose incarnate humility and weighted sense of earth are important to Russian Orthodox sensibilities. The effeminate, hands-folded, eyes-raised images of Christ which abound in Western art are completely alien in spirit to iconographic depictions, which stress a "sympathetic," "reasonable," and "courageous" image which seems to look directly at the observer.[19] This face-to-face positioning represents Christ or specific saints as "a personality entering into relationships with other personalities."[20] Bakhtin describes the personality of Christ as "the unique one" who shows mercy, "assuming the burden of sin and expiation—and all others as relieved of this burden and redeemed." This "burden" is recapitulated in Bakhtin's struggle, in his feeling that a moral life is related to an ongoing engagement in the world which is attentive to detail and particularity. And this is reflected in practice. "What I must be for the other, God is for me."[21] This can be thought about, again, in terms of the liminal space of the icon and its incarnation ethic: answerability as a practical form, in relation to an ideal. Sonia, of course, provides a Christ-like iconic presence for Raskolnikov. *She* is for Raskolnikov what *Christ* is for her. When she learns the truth of the murders, she cries out "There is no one—no one in the whole world now so unhappy as you!" It is her very compassion which implies an "inclusion" and allows Raskolnikov to reveal himself in the first place. She is a threshold figure—earth bound, yet free of those bonds—who embodies the spirit of the law rather than its letter, and provides that benevolent presence which allows Raskolnikov to be included within an iconographic ideal himself.

Raskolnikov's nihilistic ideal, on the other hand, accrues only to himself and his own turbulent personality. His isolation and his obsessive look *within* partakes of no liminal interaction or conception. Instead, he erects an *idol to self* which provides him with an unbalanced version of reality, but one which illustrates the solipsism implied in what Bakhtin called "the illusory nature of solitude." Solitude (or perhaps solitariness) is a problem for Bakhtin because "consciousness," in his view, "is in essence multiple." We proceed ethically and intellectually in the world in relation to other consciousnesses. We know who we are by our interactions with others. A character like Raskolnikov, who is monologic and narcissistic, effects a "[s]eparation, disassociation, and enclosure within the self" which become "the main reasons for the loss of one's self." Bakhtin points out that what is most important is, "Not that which takes place within, but that which takes place on the *boundary* between one's own and someone else's consciousness, on the *threshold*."[22]

Let us turn now to the Lazarus scene in *Crime and Punishment,* which prefigures Raskolnikov's emotional and spiritual resurrection (and, I would argue, makes the epilogue intrinsic to the novel as a whole). Roger Anderson considers Sonia's room an iconographic space and an example of how iconography's "technical optics" work in the novel.[23] Sonia's abode "was a large but exceedingly low pitched room . . . on the right hand wall was another door . . . it was a very irregular quadrangle and this gave it a grotesque appearance. A wall with three windows looking out on to the canal ran aslant so that one corner formed a very acute angle. . . . The other corner was disproportionately obtuse." It had "scarcely any furniture." This "form and grouping" is typical of iconographic "architecture," which is "often contrary to logic and in separate details is emphatically illogical." In icons, for example, "[d]oors and windows are often pierced in wrong places, their size does not correspond to the functions" (*Icons* 41). But this spatial perspective recapitulates the liminal world of the icon, which is difficult to visualize in realistic form and "den[ies] the reader access to the illusion of objectivity" ("The Optics of Narration" 97). Yet the depiction corresponds to the overall reality of the central figure of the icon. In this scene we see Sonia's image within an iconographic geography, which provides another version of a threshold realm. (Svidrigailov, eavesdropping in the next room, represents an opposing image. He, too, might have been included in the invitation to "come forth," but he is "walled up" according to an exaggerated and grotesque carnality—embodiment gone bad—and proceeds to commit suicide in the most desolate setting imaginable.)

The architectural details of Sonia's room also relate to the field in which Raskolnikov hides his booty. There we see a "passage leading between two blank walls to a courtyard. On the right hand, the blank unwhitewashed wall of a four storied house stretched far into the court; on the left, a wooden boarding ran parallel with it for twenty paces into the court, and then turned sharply to the left." Anderson suggests that Dostoevsky "emphasiz[es] improbable angles and flat, empty spaces, with none of the visual depth common to realistic painting" ("The Optics of Narration" 97). More important, the architectural details imply "that the action taking place . . . is outside the laws of human logic, outside the laws of earthly existence" (*Icon* 41). Thus while Raskolnikov thinks he has erased all traces of his crime in the perfect hiding place (realistically speaking), the iconographic quality of the scene emphasizes the protagonist's moral conflict, which occurs here in the shadow of the four storied house (a visual echo of the fourth floor where the murders took place and the fourth floor from which the investigation originates). Raskolnikov hides his "treasure" under a rock in a field used as a toilet, an indication of where his heart is as well.

In Sonia's room, that "rock" begins to be dislodged as Raskolnikov hears the story of the raising of Lazarus and about the removal of a large stone from the mouth of a grave so that a man might leave its confines and "come forth!" This account also implies a threshold interaction as Lazarus emerges from the grave, stressing the earthiness of the man himself. (Again, his carnality is very much to the point. Otherwise, what is a resurrection for?) In some icons depicting this scene, the onlookers cover their mouths and noses, because Lazarus, as his housewifely sister Martha notes, *stinketh*, being *four* days in the tomb. This condition, it would seem, has some relation to Raskolnikov's condition in the novel. It seems that these two scenes complement each other, not only in their iconographic perspective, but in their thematic content as well.

Frank contends that "[b]uilt into the narrative of *Crime and Punishment* is . . . a view of how it should be read, a hermeneutic of its interpretation" (*MY* 103). That

is, the supporting characters provide an interpretive function regarding the protagonist, whose interactions are "organized so as to guide the reader toward a proper
grasp of the significance of Raskolnikov's crime" (*MY* 98). This hermeneutic principle is implied in the iconographic form as well. Consider once again the Nativity
icon where the figures in the periphery of the narrative image illustrate various aspects of the central figure (while retaining their individual status and importance).
Similarly, the characters who surround Raskolnikov provide nuance and tone to
the personality of the man and his ideas, and bring them into sharper focus while
themselves remaining remarkably distinct characters. As he comes into contact
with them, Raskolnikov becomes aware—from different angles and perspective—
of the significance of his crime. This hermeneutic arrangement thus provides Dostoevsky with a way to flesh out the "unfinished" ideas of the radical theorists, and
to thicken theory into practice by noting how ideas work in the world in relation
to specific people within particular events. The "hermeneutic" characters play an
"integral part" in making the significance of Raskolnikov's radical theory apparent
and are tied, as Frank says, to the novel's "antiradical theme" (*MY* 103).

Part of this antiradical theme revolves around the denigration of the prosaic
particularity already discussed. In Bakhtin's terms, radical frameworks like nihilism
or (a less radical) utilitarianism do not consider "all the factors" (*TPA* 27)—the
specific actors and their particular contexts and the irreplaceable self in relation to
other such selves. Bakhtin typically puts his ideas into first-person formulation
in order to reiterate to the reader that "I" which suggests specificity. And it is
in the evocation of that grounded, particular being ("me") that he suggests the
groundedness and particularity of other individuals and *their* "unique and utterly
unrepeatable roles" (*TPA* 45). It is this perspective which speaks of Bakhtin's prosaic
standard, an ethic which is related, I would suggest, to his consideration of "prose
wisdom" or "prose vision."[24] It is significant that Bakhtin's discussion of "prose
wisdom" occurs in relation to a "stupidity" which occurs as a "failure to understand
languages" that are "generally accepted" and "have the *appearance* of being *universal*"
("Discourse in the Novel" 404, emphasis mine). In other words, stupidity (a harsh
word for Bakhtin) accrues from the failure to understand the moral catastrophe of
universal theories which are divorced from practice. But the opposition between
stupidity and prose wisdom in the novel "teaches the novelist how to perceive
them physically as *objects*, to see their relativity, to externalize them, to feel out
their boundaries, that is, it teaches him how to expose and structure images of
social languages" ("Discourse in the Novel" 404). Again Bakhtin stresses the visual
dimension of this expression, as abstract theory is thrown against quotidian life,
the contrast producing an image of sorts. This juxtaposition occurs, for example,
when Raskolnikov is called to the police station after the murders. He has to dress
himself and discovers that the only socks he owns are soaked with his victims'
blood. He puts a sock on, takes it off, and puts it on again. It is all he has to

wear. He wants to take comfort in this grotesque situation by noting that "this is all conditional, all relative, all merely forms." But the repulsive reality of this blood-soaked item is an expression of the contingent nature of Raskolnikov's act and reflects an almost ludicrous attempt to divorce himself from that act, based on "theoretical" dominance.

The visual and visionary power of Dostoevsky's writing as well as the ethical conceptions of Bakhtin find concomitant elements in the iconographic form. The common thematic, visual, narrative, and perspectival elements alluded to here in a rudimentary form suggest a common emphasis on embodiment, answerability, and a prosaic standard. I also posit that the iconographic perspective challenges the formulaic reading of religious discourse as monologic or authoritarian and suggests instead an active and answerable position in relation to an ideal, one that is, nevertheless, "embodiable" in the flesh. I think that Dostoevsky's fiction and Bakhtin's philosophy reflect the Christianity that puts married priests in parishes and takes note of the flesh in its yearly rhythms of fasting and feast, a Christianity which includes the earthy peasant and an enactment of Byzantine splendor. Characters like Polenka or Sonia (or Father Zossima or Alyosha Karamazov) express this prosaic ethic. They are inextricably inculcated in a peopled, physically insistent world. They regard the image of Christ and seek to embody that ideal in their actual dealings with the various and specific characters who come their way. And they evince a genuine humility. In this way they embody the inclusive perspective of the icon. Perhaps this is what Dostoevsky had in mind when he wrote in the *Crime and Punishment* notebooks: "The Orthodox point of view; what Orthodoxy consists of."[25]

I have, of course, only touched on these various subjects and have tried to suggest the outlines of a further discussion. I think that the powerful resonance of Dostoevsky's fiction and the response to it which is implied in Bakhtin's ethics find their conceptual match in the immediacy and inclusionary realm of an artistically sophisticated iconographic art. The icon embodies the ethics of incarnation and provides an inclusive plane. It pertains to a melding between theory and practice, and reflects the tendency of both writers to see the individual implied in the thought, the word made flesh. Iconography, with its emphasis on individual identity, an ennobled physical reality, threshold realms, and an inclusive perspective, provides a fruitful venue from which one can address the concerns of these writers.

Notes

This essay is adapted from my doctoral dissertation, *Murder in the Name of Theory: Theoretical Paradigms and Ethical Problems in Works by Dostoevsky, Gide and DeLillo*, Rutgers University, 1998.

1. M. M. Bakhtin, *Toward a Philosophy of the Act,* ed. Vadim Liapunov and Michael Holquist, trans. Vadim Liapunov (Austin: University of Texas Press, 1993) 7–8. Further references are to *"TPA."*

2. Mikhail Bakhtin, "The Idea in Dostoevsky," *Problems of Dostoevsky's Poetics,* ed. and trans. Caryl Emerson. (Minneapolis: University of Minnesota Press, 1984). Further references are to "Idea."

3. M. M. Bakhtin, "K filosofii postupka," *Filosofiia i sotsiologiia nauki i tekhniki* (Moscow: Nauka, 1986) 80–160.

4. Dostoevsky's skills as a writer of a "visual" text have been remarked upon by a number of critics. Bakhtin argues that the philosophical issues which concern the author "take shape" and "develop" and "begi[n] to live an authentic 'painterly' life" ("Idea" 88, 90). Dostoevsky's colleague Nikolay Strakhov noted that the author *"felt thought* with unusual liveliness," which he would "state" in "various forms, sometimes giving [them] a very sharp, graphic expression. . . . Above all, he was an artist, he thought in images." Thus Joseph Frank describes the author's work in terms of its "intellectual *physiognomy"* (Joseph Frank, *The Stir of Liberation: 1860– 1865* [Princeton, N.J.: Princeton University Press, 1986] 42). And Robert Louis Jackson suggests that Dostoevsky's "philosophical credo" is such that "moral truth" is "embodied in real visual forms" (Robert Louis Jackson, "Two Kinds of Beauty," *Dostoevsky's Quest for Form* [New Haven and London: Yale University Press, 1966] 42, 45).

5. Dostoevsky writes this in relation to his proposed work *The Life of a Great Sinner,* an idea which became incorporated into *The Devils.* (Quoted in "Idea" 98.)

6. Joseph Frank, *The Stir of Liberation: 1860–1865* (Princeton, N.J.: Princeton University Press, 1986) 51 (emphasis mine).

7. Joseph Frank, *Dostoevsky: The Miraculous Years 1865–1871* (Princeton, N.J.: Princeton University Press, 1995) 51. Further references are to *"MY."*

8. Fyodor Dostoevsky, *Crime and Punishment* (1866), trans. Constance Garnett (New York: Bantam Books, 1981) 63. Further references are to *"CP."* See also Natalia Reed, "The Philosophical Roots of Polyphony: A Dostoevskian Reading," *Critical Essays on Mikhail Bakhtin,* ed. Caryl Emerson (New York: G. K. Hall and Co., 1999) 117–52, esp. 124–32 on Dostoevsky, self-sacrifice, and self-scapegoating.

9. Robert Louis Jackson, "Philosophical Pro and Contra in Part One of *Crime and Punishment," The Art of Dostoevsky: Deliriums and Nocturnes* (Princeton, N.J.: Princeton University Press, 1981) 202.

10. Gary Saul Morson, *Narrative and Freedom: The Shadows of Time* (New Haven and London: Yale University Press, 1994) 226. Further references are to "Morson."

11. My thanks to Gerald Pirog for pointing out this note and its relevance to my theme.

12. Dostoevsky insisted that his "idealism" was "more real than [the realists'] realism." His own work is "realism, only deeper." Joseph Frank comments that Dostoevsky sees his own " 'realism' as becoming 'fantastic' because it delves beneath the

quotidian surface into the moral-spiritual depths of the human personality, while at the same time striving to incarnate a more-than-pedestrian or commonplace moral ideal" (*MY* 308–9). The name "Razumikhin," moreover, contains the word "reason" [*razum*] in Russian. Frank comments that the name "indicates Dostoevsky's desire to link the employment of this faculty not only with the cold calculations of Utilitarianism but also with spontaneous human warmth and generosity" (*MY* 99).

13. Don DeLillo, *The Names* (1982) (New York: Random House, Vintage Book edition, 1989) 290.

14. Morson 226–27. Gary Saul Morson notes that Constance Garnett omits this important part of the text in her translation, which refers to the last minutes before he commits the murders, as "he continues to do the sheer minimum necessary to keep the dream alive," as Morson says. Raskolnikov's and the peasant's "mechanical" behavior is reminiscent of Bakhtin's words in *"Art and Answerability"*: "A whole is called "mechanical" when its constituent elements are united only in space and time by some external connection and are not imbued with the internal unity of meaning. The parts of such a whole are contiguous and touch each other, but in themselves they remain alien to each other" (1). I thank Valerie Nollan for pointing out this connection to me.

15. Leonid Ouspensky and Vladimir Lossky, *The Meaning of Icons*, trans. G. E. H. Palmer and E. Kadloubovsky (Boston: Boston Book and Art Shop, Inc., 1969) 31. Further references are to *"Icon."*

16. Robert Hughes, *The Shock of the New* (New York: Alfred A. Knopf, 1991) 17.

17. Charles Lock, "Iconic Space and the Materiality of the Sign," unpublished article, 1.

18. Boris Uspensky, *The Semiotics of the Russian Icon*, ed. Stephen Rudy, trans. P. A. Reed (Lisse: Peter DeRidder Press, 1976) 38. Further references are to "Uspensky.)

19. Dostoevsky to N. D. Fonvizina, 1854, *Selected Letters of Fyodor Dostoyevsky*, ed. Joseph Frank and David I. Goldstein, trans. Andrew MacAndrew (New Brunswick, New Jersey, Rutgers University Press) 68. I use here Dostoevsky's description of the Christ with Whom he would stay even if He were a "mistake."

20. M. M. Bakhtin, "Dostoevsky's Polyphonic Novel," *Problems of Dostoevsky's Poetics*, ed. and trans. Caryl Emerson (Minneapolis: University of Minnesota Press, 1984) 31–32.

21. M. M. Bakhtin, *Art and Answerability*, ed. Michael Holquist and Vadim Liapunov, trans. Vadim Liapunov (Austin: University of Texas Press, 1990) 56.

22. M. M. Bakhtin, "Toward the Reworking of the Dostoevsky Book," *Problems of Dostoevsky's Poetics*, ed. and trans. Caryl Emerson, Theory and History of Literature, Volume 8 (Minneapolis: University of Minnesota Press, 1984) 287.

23. Roger Anderson, "The Optics of Narration: Visual Composition in *Crime*

and Punishment," Russian Narrative and Visual Art: Varieties of Seeing, ed. Roger Anderson and Paul Debreczeny (Gainesville: University Press of Florida, 1994) 95. Anderson's fascinating article prompted the direction of this paper.

24. M. M. Bakhtin, "Discourse in the Novel," *The Dialogic Imagination,* ed. Michael Holquist, trans. Caryl Emerson and Michael Holquist (Austin: University of Texas Press, 1981) 404.

25. Fyodor Dostoevsky, *The Notebooks for Crime and Punishment,* ed. and trans. Edward Wasiolek (Chicago: The University of Chicago Press, 1967) 188.

Let Us Say That There Is a Human Being before Me Who Is Suffering: Empathy, Exotopy, and Ethics in the Reception of Latin American Collaborative Testimonio

Kimberly A. Nance

Let us say that there is a human being before me who is suffering. . . . I must experience—come to see and know what he experiences; I must put myself in his place and coincide with him, as it were. (How this projection of myself into him is possible and in what form—the psychological problem of such projection—we shall not consider here. It is enough for our purposes that such projection, within certain limits, is possible in fact.) But in any event my projection of myself into him must be followed by a return into myself, a return to my own place outside the suffering person, for only from this place can the other be rendered meaningful ethically, cognitively, or aesthetically. If this return into myself did not actually take place, the pathological phenomenon of experiencing another's suffering as one's own would result—an infection with the other's suffering, and nothing more.
—Bakhtin, "Author and Hero in Aesthetic Activity," Art and Answerability

*T*estimonio as a Latin American genre is defined by a speaking subject who narrates her experience of political violence as part of a project of ameliorating social injustice. Since many of these subjects do not read and write, their access to the larger audience afforded by print is frequently mediated by professional writers. As regards reception, the early years of what has come to be known as the "testimonial moment" were characterized by euphoric celebration of a poetics of solidarity among all concerned; victory was declared as new voices contested oppressive governments' official stories. In the 1990s the tone of critical reception shifted to one of profound suspicion of motives and pessimism regarding the genre's social possibilities. Whether nostalgically, as of lost innocence, or righteously, as of revealed guilt, the testimonial moment is now spoken of in past tense. But declarations of *testimonio*'s triumph and reports of its demise both strike me as premature, and as revealing more about the genre's ability to frustrate literary and cultural critics than about *testimonio* itself.

In the first instance, when "finding a voice" was supposed to indicate or assure victory, analysis of *testimonio* effectively ended in the forum in which literary critics felt competent—the literary arena. While *testimonio's* speakers were emphatic in declaring that the project did not end with the production or even with enthusiastic reception of the text, but rather was directed toward producing change in the lifeworld, literary criticism was ill equipped to assess such effects, and responded either by reducing the project to its literary manifestation, or by a rather blithe application of the intentional fallacy—goodwill should eventually produce good social outcomes. The recent critical turn applies that same fallacy in the reverse direction—the absence of apparent social change must mean that something was fatally wrong with the *testimonio.* While these critics have broadened the focus from *testimonio* as text to *testimonio* as social project, they have in the process seriously foreshortened its time frame. Where speakers project social effects in terms of generations—Alvarado, for instance, states that it is already too late to expect change to come for her children, but that her grandchildren might see it—in 1995 a critic could condense the evidence against the efficacy of *testimonio* in one word: "Chiapas."[1] But, as a new millenium dawns, it is clear that, at least to many people in Chiapas, 1995 was not the last word.

To say more about *testimonio* and its social possibilities will require a subtlety and simultaneity that excludes neither the textual nor the social dimension of the project, an approach that resists both collapsing them into a single entity and erecting between them an insurmountable barrier. Bakhtin's work, especially in the essays that appear in the posthumous collection *Art and Answerability,* is well suited to these demands, elaborating and opening up issues of dialogue and prosaics that have either been absent or have effectively collapsed in testimonial criticism to date. Indeed, in the initial encounter that produces collaborative *testimonio,* the professional writer is situated precisely in the position postulated in the quotation from "Author and Hero in Aesthetic Activity" that opens this essay. Before her is the human being who is suffering. Her answer, in the form of the text, will set the stage for a second encounter, this time with the reader. The inviting coincidence, however, does not mean that Bakhtin's formulations can be simply "applied" to *testimonio.* Power relations are a key element of the genre, and this is an area that receives little explicit attention from Bakhtin. As Holquist points out in the introduction to *Art and Answerability,*

> While there is perhaps a greater opening toward such an enterprise [the forging of a politics] in Bakhtin's less restricted version of the others, the lack of a more carefully considered treatment of conflict and power relations in self/other dealings is something of a limitation in Bakhtin's thought as well,

particularly in these early works, in which questions of class and gender distinctions are also absent.[2]

Even as Bakhtin's work illuminates the reception of *testimonio,* analysis of the testimonial encounter to some measure returns the favor, shedding light on a point in that passage on the response to suffering. In discussing empathy, Bakhtin calls attention to the problem of empathically experiencing suffering and then "not returning to one's own place" outside it. The result, he states "would be a pathological infection with the other's suffering, and nothing more."[3] But, apart from the special case of a loved one, which is not specified and moreover of which Bakhtin usually takes notice (recall that this is merely a "human being who is suffering"), it is difficult, masochistic pleasure excepted, to see why such a lingering in suffering might take place. Why would one not hasten back to one's position outside the suffering? The meticulous attention to the specifics of positionality that is a constant in Bakhtin's work will, when focused on the special case of *testimonio,* suggest a possible answer.

Early on, both accounts of production and literary criticism focused on the achievement of empathy and quite studiously ignored the issue of exotopy in *testimonio.* Given the social and economic class differences that separate writer and speaker in collaborative *testimonio,* it stands to reason that the achievement of empathy might be problematic; exotopy perhaps less so, but instead it appears that writers' and in particular critics' responses to a difficult empathy have in turn complicated exotopy, the return of the professional writer to her own place. A great deal of critical attention was early on dedicated to the necessity of bonding between writers and narrators that coupled their voices in the production of these *testimonios,* but analysis has been hampered both by the uncritical assumption that more is better, a failure to recognize the possibly pathological dimension of empathy that Bakhtin points out.

Differences between writer and speaker are seen as obstacles to be overcome as quickly as possible, often through an assumed essentialism. According to Fernández-Olmos, "The sharing of 'women's work' [by Poniatowska and Palancares] brought together two individuals from different worlds within the same national boundaries,"[4] and "Their [Burgos and Menchú's] sharing of 'women's tasks' brought them even closer and awakened feelings which had long been forgotten."[5] It is clear from such articles that writers should not exercise what distinguishes them from speakers—their professional skills: "The editor's admiration for Menchú and her message is apparent in the minimal interference with the transcribed text."[6] It is even better if they do not possess professional skills: "Initially, I thought that knowing nothing about Rigoberta's culture would be a handicap, but it soon proved to be a positive advantage. I was able to adopt the position of someone who was learning."[7] In fact, it is generally considered to be a good sign if the writer is not only minimized but altogether disappears. "I became what I really was: Rigoberta's listener. I allowed her to speak and then became her instrument, her double, allowing her to make the transition from oral to written word."[8] Fernández-Olmos affirms:

> And for authors, it is more than a lesson in humility: the temptation to impose one's ideological viewpoint and one's own words must give way to the self-effacing skill and genius that "lets them speak" in order to appreciate the lessons of a life that is lived, and of ideas that are born of practice, even allowing for the occasional lapses into inconsistency or brilliance.[9]

Beverley notes approvingly that "Erasure of authorial presence and nonfictional character make possible a different kind of complicity—we might call it fraternal or sororal—between narrator and reader than is possible in the novel."[10]

While Hitchcock warned "The materiality of the privilege of the Western critic (like that of the novelist over her character) cannot be wished away, but neither can we be content to bandy this as an a priori, forever preserving it as an inevitable state of cultural apartheid,"[11] the former position largely prevailed. Critics effaced as well the class and cultural differences separating writer (and themselves) from narrator. To be sure, such differences were occasionally mentioned, but only to be effectively dismissed in short order. In the chronicles and criticism, it was often the professional writer, not the speaking subject, who was depicted as socially constrained and deprived, who was in need of liberation.

Interstingly, as the work progresses . . . Poniatowska's own isolation is shattered as well, the social limitation imposed on women of the privileged classes: in the example of a woman free of middle-class conventions and with whom she increasingly identifies, Poniatowska recognizes her own potential for self-affirmation and independence. . . . Poniatowska was therefore challenged by Jesusa's freer language to go beyond the prevailing taboos regarding the propriety of a woman's expression and the internalized restrictions of her own class-related limitations and expectations.[12]

> . . . the particular form of Poniatowska's work derives from the emptiness she found in her position as a woman of privilege and from her using that position to cultivate a readiness of imagination and spirit; when this readiness met with vivid exposure to the dispossessed, she converted equivocal privilege into real strength. Such an evolution would make her links to the dispossessed a continuing necessity.[13]

In this new incarnation of dependency theory, the dependent party is the upper-middle or upper-class writer. The writers' positions of privilege and power are acknowledged, only to be transformed into their opposite.

At the same time the writer is effaced, her privilege converted to lack, the converse transformation is effected on the speaker. The power of the speaker in the production of the text is magnified, even to the point of casting her attitude and relation to the writer in such negative terms as "exploitative" and "utilitarian," and the social forces that constrain her are transformed into the sources of a greater liberty: recall that while Poniatowska's membership in the middle class limits her vocabulary, Jesusa's poverty makes her "freer." Regarding the relationship between the indigenous community activist Menchú and the anthropologist, Elisabeth Burgos, who interviewed her and produced the book, Beverley observes:

> In the creation of testimonial text, control of representation does not just flow one way. . . . Someone like Menchú is also in a sense exploiting her interlocutor in order to have her story reach and influence an international audience, something that, as an activist for her community, she sees in quite utilitarian terms as a political task. Moreover, editorial power does not belong to the compiler alone.[14]

Maier expands this point: "This use of Burgos may not be 'callous,' but neither is it naïve, for she knows that her will to survive is matched (or even surpassed) by Burgos' determination to get her story into Spanish and—not incidentally—to save herself."[15] After citing a personal meeting with Menchú and the coincidence of her appearance with Burgos-Debray's description ("childlike," "guileless as a child"), Beverley draws on his own life experience to triumphantly unmask Menchú:

> But I had not spent a good part of my youth in left-wing organizations of one sort or another not to be able to recognize behind this image (which might serve as an advertisement for Guatemalan embroideries or tourist agencies) the at once inspiring and intimidating figure of the *organizer*.[16]

> What, after all, was the daughter of Mayan peasants from the Guatemalan highlands doing speaking to an audience of yuppie professors and students at New York University anyway?[17]

In the context of the university, understood both as an institution of the "West" and of class power, *testimonios* are almost literal "foreign agents"—which is why the figure of Rigoberta Menchú and the assignment of her *testimonio* in one of the courses of the Stanford general education requirement became a central focus for the neoconservative assault on multicultural education and political correctness.[18]

Menchú is thus revealed as the "intimidating figure" hiding behind a mask of guilelessness and even, by association, a "foreign agent." Burgos' characterization of Menchú's appearance as "childlike" has its own problems, among them a culture-bound perception of neoteny[19] and an invitation to patronage, but Beverley's twist on it suggests that Menchú is deliberately dissimulating.

While writers are critically enjoined from being literary, the speakers, subject to no such prohibition, can fulfill the vacated role of author. For Kerr, it is Jesusa's voice that is "independent and masterful."[20] She calls the opening quotation from Jesusa an

> oddly "literary" statement about the relation between the text that will be read and the tale she will be seen to have narrated, if not entirely authored. For it posits her absence as an inevitable ending for the dialogue between the invisible (but not necessarily audible) author and the protagonist, between the documentary researcher and the native informant. It prefigures the disappearance of the character, whose responsibility for the text may come to be regarded as equal to, if not greater than, the author who also authorizes her appearance.[21]

Speaking of the Wednesdays when Poniatowska comes to interview her, the speaker who served as model for Jesusa remarks, "*Algún día que venga ya no me va a encontrar* [Someday you'll come and you won't find me]."[22] Like the deskilling of the writer, the conversion of speaker to literary figure sometimes requires a considerable critical effort.

When class and power differences are obscured by this insistence by critics on an equality of power between writer and speaker, a trace of ambivalence sometimes remains in the qualifiers (*almost* literal foreign agents, *in a sense* exploiting, *may not be* "callous," the tale she [Jesusa] will be seen to have narrated *if not entirely* authored, whose responsibility for the text may come to be regarded as equal to, *if not greater than*, the author). While comprehensible and no doubt well intentioned as a corrective against the assumption of naïveté and lack of intelligent intentionality on the part of the speaker, the insistence on the equality of power and particularly the use of such loaded terms as "exploit," "use," and "masterful" to describe the narrator strain credulity. In just what sense are the writers being exploited, used, or mastered? What are they being forced to do against their own will and interests? As evidence of Menchú's power in the relationship, Beverley cites two facts: Menchú has chosen to keep secrets and "although Burgos-Debray does the final selection and shaping, the individual units are wholly composed by Menchú and as such depend on her skills and intentionality as a narrator."[23] The first piece of evidence is especially ironic, given the many instances of interrogation represented in Menchú's testimony. Silence in the face of questioning, withholding information, may testify to a personal ability to resist (although Scarry reminds us just how illusory is such an ability),[24] but it does not make the person questioned equal in power to the questioner. The second item of evidence is likewise unpersuasive in terms of relative possession of power. As already demonstrated, the writer was particularly reluctant to exercise such power, but it remains clear that it was her choice. Each speaker enjoys only such power over the manuscript as the writer is willing to cede. While that amount may be very large, while the writer may feel morally obligated to give up the power that literary society has vested in her, and while each speaker is a powerful orator in her own right, the power of the professional writer is undeniable and thus it comes as no surprise that Menchú should feel endangered and grateful.[25]

In contrast with the blurring of the power dynamic by writers and critics, speakers insist, repeatedly and often in the bluntest of terms, on the differences in position between themselves and the others they seek to address. Menchú keeps her distance with her secrets, and in public addresses insists that what First World readers can learn from *testimonio* is, first, to acknowledge the difference between their own privilege, power, and resources vis-à-vis those of the speakers, second, to respect those who have learned through experience, and, third, that the combination of recognizing one's own privilege and the humanity of the other leads ethically to an acknowledgment of responsibility to act on behalf of social justice. In Bakhtinian terms, the reader must be answerable. This last obligation, importantly, was to be discharged at home. "Her call was not for North Americans to change Guatemala—'We can do that,' she said—but for them to do something about North America."[26] Barrios de Chungara sharply satirizes those at the International Women's Year Tribunal who want her to "forget for a moment about the massacres" and concentrate on their mutual status as women:[27]

> Let's speak about us, *señora*, we're women. Look, *señora*, forget the suffering of your people. For a moment, forget the massacres, we've talked enough about that. We've heard you enough. Let's talk about us . . . about you and me . . . well, about women.[28]

> So I said, all right, let's talk about the two of us. But if you'll let me, I'll begin. *Señora*, I've known you for a week. Every morning you show up in a different outfit and on the other hand, I don't. Every day you show up all made up and combed like someone who has time to spend in an elegant beauty parlor and who can spend money on that, and yet I don't. And in order to show up here like you do, I'm sure you live in a really elegant home, in an elegant neighborhood, no? And yet we miners' wives only have a small house on loan to us, and when our husbands die or get sick or are fired from the company, we have ninety days to leave the house and then we're in the street.[29]

> Now *señora*, tell me: is your situation at all similar to mine? Is my situation at all similar to yours? So what equality are we going to speak of between the

two of us, if you and I are not alike, if you and I are so different we can't, at this moment, be equal, even as women, don't you think?[30]

Testimonio's speakers, then, manifested no illusions about the power relationship between themselves and the writers. The writers acknowledged their power more or less uneasily in their writing about attempts to divest themselves of it in the process of creating the text. Why should critics then have insisted on the fictions of a power equilibrium or even on an albeit benevolent "exploitation" of the writer by the speaker-narrator? At one level, such a construction might be seen as the expression of hope for a project, as if saying it is so could make it so, but the claim of equality of power where that equality does not exist in fact is less benign than the belief in a sympathetic magic that would transform words into world. Instead, it appears to be a strategic move necessitated by an extreme privileging of empathy over exotopy, accompanied by the assumption that empathy must entail identity. In this formulation, any difference between writer and narrator can only be conceived of as an obstacle: if it cannot be removed in practice, and if it cannot be overlooked, then it must be actively denied. Since literary skills and the power that accompanies a particular class position are particularly powerful and persistent differences between the writer and the speaker, their erasure will require a double task: the scale can be balanced only by both removing that skill and power from the writer and ascribing each to the speaker. One of the problems here is that in the process, the place of the writer is divested of the very tools that would enable her to make an active contribution qua professional writer (as opposed, say, to a transcriptionist or a voice recognition computer) and as a member of a privileged social class (in contrast with the contribution to be made by the speaker herself, or by the other members of the speaker's social class). The writer has no place to which to return: as a consequence of creating that empathy of identity, her functions have been transferred, her own place erased. Exotopy is thus foreclosed.

Prada Oropeza writes of *"ciertos riesgos de manipulación extraña a la del emisor real"* ("certain risks of manipulation apart from that of the actual speaker"),[31] and such risks cannot be discounted, but this "manipulation" of words can also be a professional writer's legitimate contribution to the collaborative effort—her potential usefulness to the cause lies precisely in her difference, her skill, and social position, in Bakhtinian terms, in the "ever-present excess of [her] seeing, knowing, and possessing in relation to any other human being . . . founded in the uniqueness and irreplaceability of [her] place in the world."[32] If this difference is effaced in the quest for a pathological and ultimately illusory empathic identity, the possibilities of dialogic action are correspondingly diminished. By converting an address to someone with the power to help into a "sororal" conversation with a covictim of oppression, *testimonio* becomes not a call to action but rather another addition to the growing shelf of self-help volumes. Alternatively, taking up a position of assumed solidarity beside the speaker as she "talks back to power," rather than remaining oneself within her field of address, allows for a gratifying feeling of purity, without having to take responsibility for one's own privileged position; thus *testimonio* can be catalogued as if the message were addressed to someone else, an evil other. Either reading makes *testimonio* comfortably consumable rather than ethically challenging.

In the early era of testimonial criticism, reading itself became an expression of solidarity, blurring not only the boundaries among reader, writer, and speaker, but also between textworld and lifeworld. Sommer observed, "to read women's testimonials, curiously, is to mitigate the tension between First World self and Third World other. I do not mean this as a license to deny the differences, but as a suggestion that the testimonial subject may be a model for respectful nontotalizing politics."[33] But if the testimonial subject is indeed to be taken as a model, it should be noted that a key part of what she is modeling is precisely a keen awareness of difference, which should, in her own estimation, produce a tension that the reader could mitigate only through social action, not through reading. Alvarado speaks clearly to this point:

> But if you sit around thinking what to do and end up not doing anything, why bother even thinking about it? You're better off going out on the town and having a good time. No, we have to think and act. That's what we're doing here, and that's what you have to do. I hate to offend you, but we won't get anywhere by just writing and reading books.
>
> I know that books are important, and I hope this book is important for people who read it. But we can't just read and say "Those poor *campesinos*. What a miserable life they have." Or others might say "What a nice book. That woman Elvia sounds like a nice woman." I imagine there'll be others who say "That Elvia is a foul-mouthed, uppity *campesina*." But the important thing is not what you think of me, the important thing is that you do something.[34]

The "you" here is not a government or a political party, but instead a specific address to the reader herself, one who is reminded of her options to act or not, to assist in the project or "go out on the town." Joining the speaker in that project is one of her options: the promise of alliance is offered only through action, not through reading and contemplation. Speakers specifically addressed readers, including writers and critics, but the latter, albeit with aspirations of a "poetics of solidarity," effectively refused this address when they fused with the speaker rather than listening to her. What speakers requested of the readers, and what they offered them in return, was not the high drama of a poetics, a shortcut to the sublime, but rather something closer to what Moreiras seems to be referring to as "subdued sublime,"[35] a *prosaics* in Morson and Emerson's term,[36] of solidarity, one founded on considered, contingent, concrete, and undramatic actions in every-day life.

By insisting not only on difference, but moreover on the maximal specificity and on the enabling value of both positions, one's own as well as the others, by pointing out the limits to useful empathy and the pathological dimension of its extension, and by grounding questions of ethics in the quotidian and small-scale encounter, a Bakhtinian formulation of the testimonial encounter offers a revealing contrast with the illusory fusions described above, a more useful model for the writer's or reader's participation in the projects of alliance politics—and one which also recuperates the speaker's own formulations. Paradoxically, it is Bakhtin's emphasis on the uniquely enabling as well as ultimately inescapable position of the self that helps to recuperate *testimonio*'s call to action on behalf of the other. Among the practical implications of this analysis are the revisions of paratexts and particularly prologues so that they acknowledge and value exotopy as well as empathy, emphasizing the difference and potential of the reader's position in contrast with that of the speaker, and the critical examination of *testimonio* in terms of prosaics, rather than poetics. As Foucault has pointed out, commentary is an effort to channel readings in certain directions,[37] and so far, it must be observed, the paratexts produced by *testimonio*'s collaborating writers and critics, not to mention teachers who assign these works in classes, have tended to channel readers into easy empathy, rather than exotopy or action.

That this empathy, adoption of the position of cosufferer, should in certain cases be the easier path illustrates the means by which an acknowledgment of class and power differences productively complicates (without contradicting) Bakhtin's theorization of response to suffering. In this formula, pain is associated most directly with the condition of empathy. No mention is made of a cause for the human being's suffering, and most notably, there is no indication that the "I" of the passage is in any way responsible, whether through commission or omission, for that suffering. For that matter, neither is it specified whether the human being somehow deserved to suffer, a possibility that Bakhtin explicitly acknowledges in *Toward a Philosophy of the Act* with a reference to "the destruction and completely jus-tified disgrace of a person."[38] But what happens when the specifics of the situation are spelled out, a step that Bakhtin in that same essay insists is a requirement of any ethical judgement: "There *is* no acknowledged self-equivalent and universally valid value, for its acknowledged validity is conditioned *not* by its content, taken in abstraction, but by its being *correlated* with the unique place of a participant."[39] What if it turns out that the "I" is, while not deliberately hurtful, culpably negligent in terms of her social responsibility; and further, that the suffering human being has done nothing to deserve her fate?

Here the choice is not between a painful empathy and a presumably less painful exotopy. On the contrary, both positions are now invested with a certain quantity of pain—empathy with a pain coexperienced through identification and importantly undeserved, and exotopy with another sort of pain, namely guilt. When the choice is between joining imaginatively in the suffering of the innocent or experiencing the pangs of one's own conscience, the appeal of the former is small wonder. The possibility of this response is apparently not lost on *testimonio's* speakers, who in an anticipatory countermove, often employ the same trope used by Las Casas in his address to the Catholic monarchs in Spain regarding the abuses of indigenous peoples in the New World—you must not have known about this situation, or about your capacity to remedy it, or else you would have done something about it[40]—thus offering access to a renewed innocence to salve the potential pain of the exotopic position.

If in the celebratory response to *testimonio* writers, critics and readers were too ready to deny difference between the text and the lifeworld, and in particular between their own privilege and the oppression of others, the moment of mourning was heralded, at its extremes, by precisely the opposite set of responses. The dissolution of boundaries was replaced by their assiduous and unequivocal reinstatement. Not only were reading and writing not revolution, which in itself might have been a useful starting point, but it was declared highly dubious, if not impossible, that literature might influence life. " . . . [I]n dealing with *testimonio*, I have also begun to discover in myself a kind of posthumanist agnosticism about literature."[41] Not only were the speakers clearly different from writers, critics, and readers in terms of class position, but they were so incommensurably so that communication across the divide was probably impossible. Colás finds the "resonance and reach" of *testimonio* "unimaginable to those of us in the First World today."[42] Rather than automatic allies in unquestionable solidarity, readers, writers, and critics themselves posed a danger from which Sommer suggested that vulnerable speakers needed to be cordoned off;[43] the most responsible tack the former might take, presumably, was to step back from that rope. Reading *testimonio* from the First World, one could only watch in incomprehension or, in other formulations, grief. Georg Gugelberger concludes his introduction to the 1996 essay collection, *The Real Thing: Testimonial Discourse and Latin America,* with the words: "we may not like this outcome but we can hardly avoid its implications. In the end there is only 'mourning,' 'travail du deuil' as Jacques Derrida has called it, or the famous 'Trauerarbeit' of which Walter Benjamin already has spoken."[44]

While such responses hold out the attractive propositions of hardheaded political pragmatism and intense respect for difference, distancing themselves from the illusory idealism and appropriative fusion of their precursors, it must be noted that the third wave take on *testimonio*[45] (like third-wave feminism?) has a similar, and arguably even stronger, more chilling effect on the likelihood of reader participation in *testimonio's* social project. When not mistaking readng for social action, readers who naïvely saw themselves in solidarity with the speaker might occasionally, even if equally naïvely, be induced to participate in social projects. Savvy third-wave readers, on the other hand, know better than to believe that testimonial writing, or they themselves, for that matter, can contribute to social justice. They've learned to keep a safe and socially responsible distance between themselves and *testimonio*.

To question the latest positions might be dismissed as merely a lingering nostalgia for that celebratory moment, a stubborn unwillingness to accept the reality that *testimonio* is a failure. Literary critics are hardly immune to denial. Nevertheless, the current trend appears to fetishize boundaries as strongly as the previous one denied them—and to offer readers alibis on grounds that are equally untenable. A key underpinning rests on the apparently empirical finding that despite volumes of *testimonio*, an uprising in Chiapas can still be unsuccessful. Admittedly, I am to some extent polemicizing by localizing to the case of Chiapas—as, I expect, was Beverley in his single-word refutation—but even more extensive evidence of continued social injustice and failed revolution is not enough to prove the impossibility of the testimonial project—not on the speaker's own terms, and certainly not on the revolutionary time scale envisioned by theorists such as Rosa Luxemburg, who saw even failed movements as useful and perhaps even necessary preliminaries to eventual change.[46] The First World expectation of immediate gratification seems to extend even to the appetite for social justice. But if it is still too early to expect empirical proof of *testimonio's* efficacy, how can we know whether *testimonio* might not be a blind alley, diverting time and energy from what might be more productive strategies for social change?

This brings us to the possible connection between literature and life, another area in which Bakhtin's penchant for exploring the both/and offers a fruitful alternative to category collapse or Manichean binaries. As Holquist points out, "literary texts are tools: they serve as a prosthesis of the mind. As such, they have a tutoring capacity that materially effects change by getting from one stage of development to another." "Literature," he claims, "enables the future to be exploited as a zone of proximal development." It has "a particularly important role to play in the economy of dialogism, then, because it affords opportunities of a unique power to explore, to teach possibilities of authorship. . . . Literature is essentially a perceptual activity, a way to see the world that enriches the world's communicability."[47] Seen in these terms, while *testimonio* cannot change the world directly, it does offer readers a means of changing their minds about the world, a development which may, in turn, lead to activism. Or it may not, and this is another area in which Bakhtin's subtlety is a useful antidote to either euphoria or despair regarding *testimonio's* social possibilities. The locus of action remains the place of the individual reader, for whom the work itself is only one of many sources of information to be considered when contemplating action, a position not unknown to testimonial speakers: "So I've learned that if you want to know what's going on in the world, you should study as much as you can. You should read or listen to the news as much as you can. You should take it all in, but digest it in your own way, and judge for yourself what you think the truth is."[48] Certainly the notion of optimally effective socially engaged writings as that which would somehow automatically lead to good social action (a quality once ascribed to *testimonio*) by all those who chanced to read it is a seductive one. Against such a notion, *testimonio* would have to be judged an abysmal failure.

Upon reflection, however, it becomes apparent why any such irresistible consummation of reading is not an outcome devoutly to be wished. As framed in a conversation in a 1995 Bakhtin seminar led by Caryl Emerson, to posit the ideal book that could have forestalled a Holocaust carries with it as a corollary another possible book that could start another. Not only is the reader's response to literature less than certain, but that is not a bad thing. If dreams that *testimonio* could end oppression were misguided, so too are assertions of literature's definitive inefficacy. While not irresistible, a text that addresses and makes demands of a reader can under certain conditions serve to catalyze a potential for action. As Bakhtin noted in his earliest extant essay "Art and Answerability" (1919), "art and life are not one, but they must become united in me, in the unity of my responsibility."[49]

As a politically engaged genre that seeks a social response from its readers, *testimonio* confronts readers with that *potential* unity and consequent responsibility in a particularly intense way. However, as apparent in the controversy sparked by David Stoll's *Rigoberta Menchú and the Story of All Poor Guatemalans*, which appeared in 1998 alongside Menchú's second book, *Crossing Borders*, the tendency to evade that responsibility is similarly intense.[50] While conceding that the Guatemalan military did engage in widespread and violent oppression of indigenous populations, Stoll argues that many of the specifics of Menchú's narrative are untrue, and that much of the local violence was a product of family land disputes rather than government oppression. In an analytical survey of the critical responses, Arturo Arias notes that Stoll's own book is vulnerable to critique on various methodological grounds, but the ensuing debate largely ignored specific questions of method and fact.[51] Instead, it ranged at the extremes from indignation at any critical scrutiny of *Me llamo Rigoberta Menchú* to calls for its removal from university reading lists on grounds of untruthfulness. Some critics who saw themselves as taking Menchú's side argued that fact checking was essentially irrelevant to a work of literature, or that Western logic was incommensurate with Menchú's indigenous worldview. All of these responses seek to evade that demanding contingency of the unity of art and life in the choices of the reader. Whether they assert that the link is readymade (uncritical acceptance of either Menchú's account or Stoll's), or that it is impossible (assertions that either literature or indigenous thought is incommensurate with critical examination of concrete circumstance), such positions serve to absolve readers of the responsibility that both Bakhtin and Alvarado identified: the ineluctably personal obligation to learn as much as possible, to judge what the truth is, and to act accordingly.

Testimonio's speakers have shown themselves willing to wager on the reader's potential response, and I for one am loath to contradict them, particularly since we have yet to see what might happen if collaborating writers and critics were to acknowledge and employ their own skills to endorse and even to insist upon the same fundamental propositions set forth by speakers: that the speaker is in fact addressing the specific human being who is reading the text, that those readers (writers and critics included) enjoy more power and privilege than most people in the world, and that such readers have both the capacity and the concomitant responsibility to act ethically on the knowledge of injustice. Until then, the only thing that can be ascertained about the potential of *testimonio* is the speakers' limited capacity unilaterally to overcome a literary and cultural apparatus that has redirected their messages away from their intended addressees, defined and excused those addressees as incompetent or unworthy to participate in the project, and recast that project as either already complete or probably impossible. It remains to be seen what a fully collaborative *testimonio*, one in which each participant brings to bear all of the potential of her own unique position and one which insists unequivocally on both the addressability and answerability of the reader, might look like, let alone what it might accomplish in the realm of social justice.

Notes

Epigraph: Mikhail Bakhtin, "Author and Hero in Aesthetic Activity," in *Art and Answerability.* Ed. Michael Holquist and Vadim Liapunov, trans. Vadim Liapunov (Austin: University of Texas Press, 1990), 25–26. Italics original.

1. Elvia Alvarado, *Don't Be Afraid, Gringo. A Honduran Woman Speaks from the Heart,* trans. and ed. Medea Benjamin (San Francisco: Institute for Food Development Policy, 1987), John Beverley, "The Real Thing," in *The Real Thing: Testimonial Discourse and Latin America,* ed. Georg Gugelberger (Durham: Duke University Press, 1996), 282.

2. Michael Holquist, Introduction, *Art and Answerability,* xxxix.

3. Bakhtin, "Author and Hero," in *Art and Answerability,* 26.

4. Margarita Fernández Olmos, "Latin American Testimonial Narrative, or Women and the Art of Listening," *Revista Canadiense de Estudios Hispánicos* 3, no. 2 (Invierno 1989): 188.

5. Ibid., 190.

6. Ibid., 191.

7. Elisabeth Burgos-Debray, Introduction to Rigoberta Menchú, *I. Rigoberta Menchú*, ed. Elisabeth Burgos-Debray, trans. Ann Wright (London: Verso, 1984), xix.

8. Ibid., xx.

9. Fernández-Olmos, "Latin-American Testimonial," 193–94.

10. John Beverley, "'The Margin at the Center' on *Testimonio*," *Modern Fiction Studies* 35, no. 1 (spring 1989): 11–28. Reprinted in *Against Literature* (Minneapolis: University of Minnesota Press, 1993), 77.

11. Peter Hitchcock, *Dialogics of the Oppressed* (Minneapolis: University of Minnesota Press, 1993), 49.

12. Fernández-Olmos, "Latin American Testimonial," 189.

13. Bell Gail Chevigny, "The Transformation of Privilege in the Work of Elena Poniatowska" in *Faith of a (Woman) Writer*, ed. Alice Kessler-Harris and William McBrien (New York: Greenwood Press, 1988), 210.

14. Beverley, "Margin," in *Against Literature*, 21.

15. Carol Maier, "Notes after Words: Looking Forward Retrospectively at Translation and (Hispanic and Luso-Brazilian) Feminist Criticism," *Cultural and Historical Grounding for Hispanic and Luso-Brazilian Feminist Literary Criticism*, ed. Hernán Vidal (Minneapolis, Minn.: Institute for the Study of Ideologies and Literature, 1989), 637.

16. Beverley, "Margin," in *Against Literature*, 21.

17. Ibid., 90.

18. Ibid., 90.

19. As the biologist and essayist Stephen Jay Gould explains in "To Show an Ape," in *The Flamingo's Smile* (New York: W. W. Norton, 1985) neoteny is "literally, holding on to youth," the juvenile appearance of an adult organism (276). It should be noted that the perception of Menchú as looking like a child depends very much on European visual expectations—Menchú's head shape and facial features are quite normal for those of her own ethnic group.

20. Lucille Kerr, *Reclaiming the Author: Figures and Fictions from Spanish America* (Durham: Duke University Press, 1992), 57.

21. Ibid., 50.

22. Elena Poniatowska, *Hasta no verte, Jesús mío*, 1969 (México: Era, 1979), 1. Translation mine.

23. Beverley, "Margin," in *Against Literature*, 21.

24. Elaine Scarry, *The Body in Pain: The Making and Unmaking of the World* (New York: Oxford, 1985), 29–30.

25. Maier, "Notes," in Vidal, *Cultural and Historical Grounding*, 637.

26. Mary Louise Pratt, "*Me llamo Rigoberta Menchú*: Autoethnography and the Recoding of Citizenship," in *Teaching and Testimony*, ed. Allen Carey-Webb and Stephen Benz (Albany: SUNY Press, 1996), 71.

27. Domitila Barrios de Chungara and Moema Viezzer. *Si me permiten hablar* (Mexico: Siglo XXI, 1977), translated *Let Me Speak!* ed. Moema Viezzer, trans. Victoria Ortiz (New York: Monthly Review, 1978), 202.

28. Ibid., 202.

29. Ibid., 202

30. Ibid., 203

31. Renato Prada Oropeza, "De lo testimonial al *testimonio*, " in Jara and Vidal, *Cultural and Historical Grounding*, 17. Translation mine.

32. Mikhail Bakhtin, "Author and Hero," in *Art and Answerability*, 23.

33. Doris Sommer, "Rigoberta's Secrets," *Latin American Perspectives* 18 (1991), 50.

34. Alvarado, *Don't Be Afraid*, 146.

35. Alberto Moreiras, "The Aura of *testimonio*," in Gugelberger, *The Real Thing*, 195.

36. Gary Saul Morson and Caryl Emerson, *Mikhail Bakhtin: Creation of a Prosaics* (Stanford: Stanford University Press, 1990), 15.

37. Michel Foucault, "The Order of Discourse," in *Untying the Text*, ed. Robert Young (Boston: Routledge, 1981), 58.

38. Mikhail Bakhtin, *Toward a Philosophy of the Act*, trans. Vadim Liapunov, ed. Vadim Liapunov and Michael Holquist (Texas: University of Texas Press, 1993), 62.

39. Ibid., 48. Italics original.

40. Bartolomé de las Casas, *Brevísima relación de la destucción de las indias*, ed. André Saint-Lu (Madrid: Cátedra, 1984), 71.

41. Beverley, "Second Thoughts," in *Against Literature*, 99.

42. Santiago Colás, *Postmodernity in Latin America* (Durham: Duke University Press, 1994), 172.

43. Doris Sommer, "No secrets," in Gugelberger, *The Real Thing*, 136.

44. Georg M. Gugelberger, "Institutionalization of Transgression: Testimonial Discourse and Beyond," Introduction to Gugelberger, *The Real Thing*, 18.

45. Gugelberger notes the three stages: (1) *testimonio* as a Latin American phenomenon, (2) "progressive intellectual response in the US," and (3) struggle with issues of "lo real," refutation of presumed "left" poetics of solidarity and going "beyond the unconditional affirmation of the genre," ibid., 5.

46. Luxemberg's perspective is discussed in Slavoj Zizek, *The Sublime Object of Ideology* (London: Verso, 1989), 59–60, 84.

47. Michael Holquist, Introduction, *Art and Answerability*, 83–85.

48. Alvarado, *Don't Be Afraid*, 64.

49. Mikhail Bakhtin, "Iskusstvo i otvetstvennost" [Art and Responsibility] in *Voprosy literatury i estetiki: Issledovaniia let* (Moscow: Khudozhestvennaia literatura,

1975), 6. Quoted and translated in Morson and Emerson, *Mikhail Bakhtin: Creation of a Prosaics,* 32.

50. For more on the forms of reader resistance, and on the means by which testimonial speakers have sought to overcome it, see my essay "Speakers' Resistance to Readers' Defenses in Latin American *testimonio.*" *Biography* 24:3 (summer 2001): 570–88.

51. Arias offers an analytical survey of the various positions in the debate in "Rigoberta Menchú and the Performative Production of the Subaltern Self," *PMLA* 116:1 (January 2001): 75–88.

Russia as a Chronotope in Works by Ruralist Writers: Toward a Philosophy of the Art

Valerie Z. Nollan

This essay represents a convergence of two bodies of ideas that I have been pondering over the years: Russian nationalist views in works by ruralist writers,[1] and Bakhtin's concept of the chronotope. What I set out to investigate is why the image of Russia, presented variously in three literary works, emerges as a powerful unifying element, and how it functions as a chronotope. I consider works by three writers and offer a discussion of Russia as a chronotope in them; my argument takes into account Bakhtin's conceptualization of the chronotope both as a physical intersection of time and space (as experienced by the individual) and as a creative force unto itself (Mihailovic 47). Moreover, I connect the creative process of Russian nationalist writers with their product—literature containing Russia as a chronotope—by means of Bakhtin's concepts of "answerability" (*otvetstvennost'*) and the "individually answerable act" (*postupok*). The works in question are the novel *Tsar'-Ryba* (Queenfish, 1976) by Viktor Astafiev, the novella *Proshchanie s Materoi* (Farewell to Matyora, 1976) by Valentin Rasputin, and the poetic cycle "Druz'iam" (To my friends, 1990) by Vladimir Soloukhin.[2] To this corpus I apply Bakhtin's early philosophical writings—the article "Iskusstvo i otvetstvennost'" (Art and answerability, 1919) and the fragment later titled "K filosofii postupka" (Toward a philosophy of the act, 1919–21)—and the literary essay "Formy vremeni i chronotopa v romane" (Forms of time and of the chronotope in the novel, 1937–38).[3] I propose that Bakhtin's elaboration of "answerability" and the "act" can lead to a better understanding of Russia as a chronotopic idea in works by ruralist writers.[4] To provide a useful framework for a discussion of Russian nationalism, I link Bakhtin's "answerability," the "act," and the chronotope to ruralist writing through a cognitive typology elaborated by Kathleen Parthé. Parthé's typology characterizes physical and psychological space (which are suggested in Bakhtin's definition of the chronotope) in the context of how Russian thinkers understand Russian national identity; within such a typology it may be easier for us to observe and discuss the convergence of theoretical concerns in the present text. Perhaps what will emerge is a fresh look at ruralist works in light of their recoding of Russian nationalism onto a specifically understood answerability.

A question may arise regarding the connection among the concepts of answerability, the act, and ruralist poetry and prose *as* literature of Russian nationalism. To be sure, all writers write from some basic position of answerability. How, then, can we clarify what it means to Village Prose writers? Can we produce evidence from Bakhtin's philosophy and literary theory that would accurately describe the Village Prose writers' particular understanding and experiencing of answerability and the act in their relationship to the creative process? This essay has been developed on the assumption that, indeed, a fruitful link exists between Bakhtin and Village Prose. The notion of answerability (in Bakhtin's special definition of it) may be viewed as a motivating force for Village Prose writers who were concerned with recording a cherished and rapidly disappearing past, one they felt was an important repository of traditional Russian values. However, the Village Prose writers aimed for more than the creation of literary documentaries of the Russian village, and (when one considers the problems faced by artists living in the Soviet Union in the 1950s and 1960s) their aspirations may be considered courageous, even revolutionary:

> . . . one may say that [the Village Prose writers] studied, not concrete situations from a peasant world that was disappearing, or the specific character types of village inhabitants; rather, what they studied was agricultural civilization as a possible foundation, prototype, and model for the future restructuring of the world.[5]

Village Prose writers typically reworked autobiographical material into literary form as an artistic response of answerability, to their own conscience and to the collective recollection of their readers. The ethical relationships in this process approximate those in Bakhtin's consideration of the act:

> An act must acquire a single unitary plane to be able to reflect itself in both directions—in its sense or meaning and in its being; it must acquire the unity of two-sided answerability—both for its content (special answerability) and for its Being (moral answerability). And the special answerability, moreover, must be brought into communion with the unitary and unique moral answerability as a constituent moment in it. That is the only way whereby the pernicious non-fusion and non-interpenetration of culture and life could be surmounted. Every thought of mine, along with its content, is an act or deed that I perform—my own individually answerable act or deed. (*TPA* 2–3)

The answerable act or deed alone surmounts anything hypothetical, for the answerable act is, after all, the actualization of a decision—inescapably, irremediably, and irrevocably. . . . The performed act constitutes a going out *once and for all* from within possibility as such into *what is once-occurrent.* (*TPA* 28–29, emphasis original)

Bakhtin's elaboration of the act, whether prompted by lived life or created art, occurs within a philosophical and christological context. In her article on the "threshold" chronotope in Henry James's writings, Lisa Eckstrom points out,[6]

Here Bakhtin's distinction between abstract cognition and living artistic perception (a perception that incorporates all that Kant would dismiss in matters of moral judgment) finds application. . . . In *Toward a Philosophy of the Act* . . . Bakhtin's central concern is . . . to ground Kant's categorical imperative in the particulars and concreteness of an individual life. He wants what most philosophers deem impossible: to detranscendentalize Kant while preserving ethical judgment from relativism. (102)

Whether or not Bakhtin successfully "detranscendentalized" Kant is outside the scope of this essay, but his ability to preserve ethics from relativism (and theoretism) rests in large part on his retaining as addressee and interlocutor an Other consciousness (which he terms variously), for whom the worth of the *concrete* (in *this* time and *this* place), individual human being is absolute.

For Village Prose writers the act of writing about their past represented both individual artistic self-expression and a collective, deeply felt love for their homeland; consequently, a literature of patriotism became an act of particular artistic and cultural answerability.[7] In Bakhtin's words, this answerability is bound up with the "subjective experiencing" of Russia as a "once-occurrent" homeland: his discussion of Italy for the characters of Pushkin's poem "Parting" (*TPA* 65–75) crystallizes in many ways the existential positioning of the Village Prose writers vis-à-vis their writing and their country: "The experiencing of Italy as event includes, as a necessary constituent moment, the actual unity of Italy in unitary and once-occurrent Being. But this unitary Italy gains body . . . only from my affirmed participation in once-occurrent Being, in which the once-occurrent Italy is a constituent moment" (71). The ethical component of the aesthetic act emerges only from the writers' "affirmed participation" in a highly personalized, unrepeatable flow of events: once-occurrent Being. For them, the Bakhtinian ethics apprehended through the lens of a participating subject were translated into a childhood past lived in the Russian village, a present in which the autobiographical raw material was carefully sifted to yield those moments that were both typical and aesthetically viable, and a future they desired to transform by means of the "act" of their lived life and aesthetic response to it.

This artistic self-expression, what Bakhtin calls "aesthetic seeing" (*èsteticheskoe videnie*) (*TPA* 64), produced works of such power precisely because of the artists' emotional relationship with their subject matter. Bakhtin underscores:

> Lovelessness, indifference, will never be able to generate sufficient power to slow down and *linger intently* [*napriazhenno zamedlit'*] over an object, to hold and sculpt every detail and particular in it, however minute. Only love is capable of being aesthetically productive; only in correlation with the loved is fullness of the manifold possible. (*TPA* 64, emphasis original)

Gary Saul Morson reminds us, "Love is a prosaic way of knowing the specific. One does not love the instantiation of a principle. Love allows us to learn and to appreciate things inaccessible to the theoretist mind" (71).[8] On every level Bakhtin's ethics frame love in the context of specificity (a chronotopic lingering over the object of desire) and of memory (lingering takes place because the subject strives to commit the image of the loved one to memory).

The process of "lingering intently," lovingly over an aesthetic work produces in the case of Village Prose the characteristic "radiant"[9] past that permeates the writing of that literary school. Its articulators "lingered intently" by their immersion of the reader into the everyday minute details, atmosphere, and linguistic patterns of village life, which they knew intimately. The nostalgic "radiance" in their works, however, was coupled with the commitment to aesthetic propriety and transformational effect on the future. Tsvetov states:

> . . . it is impossible to maintain that [Village Prose] idealizes and elevates the past. Admires? Yes. But this admiration is determined by a strict critical selection of material. In other words, [in Village Prose] the writer is attracted only to that material from life which is worthy of admiration and which may serve future generations, not only as an ethnographic reproduction of the past, but also as a wellspring for the culture of the future. (30)

Tsvetov's term *"liubovat'sia"* with respect to Village Prose embraces the concepts of "admiration" and of "steeping oneself" in the essence of an object, meanings very close to Bakhtin's characterization of love as the state or process of "lingering intently" over an object.

Village Prose writers described with great sincerity this "radiant" past (as constituting what Parthé terms a "moral and personal truth" of the artist) of traditional Russian country life, but in doing so they also reinforced the image of

Mother Russia ubiquitous in Russian folklore and recreated an image of Russia that resonates powerfully in contemporary Russia's search for its own identity. This image remains as relevant today as it was in the 1950s. Not surprisingly, the nostalgic image of Russia in ruralist literature becomes a major contribution by these writers to the process of cultural and national mythmaking. The image of Russia, as seen through the eyes of such writers as Astafiev, Rasputin, and Soloukhin, is also chronotopic: it interacts richly with both space and time, yet finds a physical home in the pages of literature *and* in specific geographic spaces. Mihailovic notes:

> . . . for Bakhtin the chronotope represents more than merely the crossroads of human experience . . . it is a force that creates. Bakhtin is quite specific in indicating that the concretization takes place within the chronotope and is not the chronotope itself, which is actually the force that enables the embodiment he describes. (47)

In the literature under consideration, the nexus for this force happens to be the Russian village as a microcosm of Russia. Village Prose works exemplify that Russia exists as a cultural construct made viable in each individual's mind through centuries of religious, literary, and socio-political activities that have contributed various aspects to the country's identity—one transmitted and modified from one generation to the next.

Astafiev, Rasputin, and Soloukhin all consider themselves Russian nationalists, or Russian patriots (to use Dmitrii Likhachev's less politically charged term),[10] and their writings have been linked with the views of the *vozrozhdentsy*, the so-called renaissance nationalists.[11] For these three writers as avowed Russian (and also, in the case of Astafiev and Rasputin, Siberian) patriots, Russia occupies a central place in their thinking and their literary progeny. They are concerned with recording her past, refiguring her past identity, and commenting at great length in literary form on the deplorable state in which they feel Russia's culture currently finds itself. Embedded in this body of literature is a criticism of the Soviet state and its promethean policies toward the former republics, and especially, as the Russian nationalists maintain, toward Russia and most things that represented Russia's prerevolutionary past.

The model of Russia that Astafiev, Rasputin, and Soloukhin have internalized is steeped in the country's "radiant past" (*svetloe proshloe*), as Parthé explains:

> Nostalgia in literature, when not used superficially, can be a complex emotion, even a spiritual quality. It always involves a sense of sadness at loss, but a sadness that is leavened by a "radiance" or "luminousness," what Russians express with the words *svetlost'* and *svetlyi*. . . . The radiant past (*svetloe proshloe*), radiant memory (*svetlaia pamiat'*), and radiant/luminous sadness (*svetlaia pechal'*)

are central to Village Prose—as they are to other memory oriented literature.
(*Russian Village Prose* 10)

In the given works by Astafiev, Rasputin, and Soloukhin, however, there emerges by contrast with this "radiant past" a disillusionment with, even horror at, the present. This quality looms largest in Soloukhin's poetic cycle, in part because most of its poems were written during the 1980s, when Village Prose became more publicistic in its purpose (the works in question by Astafiev and Rasputin were written and published in the 1970s), and in part because of the rehistoricizing of Lenin, a process that informed Soloukhin's work at the time. After the peak of Village Prose in the late 1970s, to be sure, the ruralist writers continued writing, but some of their output of the 1980s is characterized by bitterness, anger, and resentment.[12] In many Village Prose works of the 1980s the "childhood village home" (*Malaia Rodina*) becomes Russia, with the attendant nationalist and sociopolitical (publicistic) concerns. Soloukhin's poetry must be viewed against this background.

Before attempting to locate Russia as a chronotope within the given works, we must consider Bakhtin's concept of the chronotope, a concept well known and much celebrated in the literary world. One might ask why works by ruralist writers lend themselves to an examination in light of the Bakhtinian chronotope. After all, Bakhtin concentrated the bulk of his literary analyses on pre-twentieth-century prose, while the first works of the Village Prose literary school appeared in the mid 1950s.[13] The answer lies in a closer examination of the style and thematics of Village Prose, which establish this body of work as a natural successor to nineteenth-century Russian realist novels. Both Bakhtin, in his admiration of the nineteenth-century Russian novel, and the ruralist writers, who rejected the future oriented and contrived literature of socialist realism, harkened back to the same literary phenomenon: classical realist prose crafted with the standards of art, rather than extra-artistic guiding principles, in mind. Thus it makes eminent sense for us to apply the chronotope to this post-Stalinist body of literature in particular.[14]

In his essay, "Forms of Time and of the Chronotope in the Novel," Bakhtin describes the chronotope as follows:

[It refers to] the intrinsic connectedness of temporal and spatial relationships that are artistically expressed in literature. . . .

In the literary artistic chronotope, spatial and temporal indicators are fused into one carefully thought-out, concrete whole. Time, as it were, thickens, takes on flesh, becomes artistically visible; likewise, space becomes charged and responsive to the movements of time, plot, and history. This intersection of axes and fusion of indicators characterizes the artistic chronotope.

. . . The chronotope as a formally constitutive category determines to a significant degree the image of man in literature as well. The image of man is always intrinsically chronotopic. (84–85)

The chronotope, in its incarnations both as a "crossroads of human experience" and a "force that creates," enabling the concretization of the individually experienced event, remains a slippery concept whose applicability to literature runs the risk of producing a circular argument: in the present case, one may say that Village Prose writing on Russia is chronotopic because Russia linguistically and metaphorically falls within Bakhtin's extended, though broad characterizations of the chronotope. Although this problem should not present the enterprising literary critic from foraying into uncharted territory and making well-reasoned connections, further attempts to systematize the meaning-laden chronotope would be indicated. To this end, in his groundbreaking article which yields significant insights into the "legibility" of the chronotope for literary analysis, Jay Ladin notes,[15]

This circularity grows out of the tendency to refer to a chronotope as though it were a thing, a noun, a bounded entity—whereas it is, as Bertrand Russell said of electricity, not so much a thing as a way things happen. By being enacted within a particular kind of space-time, abstract narrative information (e.g., who did what to whom) is transformed into specific, meaning- and value-charged images. At the same time, the chronotope becomes significant through its association with narrative events. . . .

. . . In other words, from the reader's point of view, chronotopes become "visible" by comparison with other kinds of space-time." (219)

One point to consider regarding Bakhtin's chronotope is how it differs from a symbol, image, or metaphor: the chronotope is conceptually larger and broader than these devices, and can take all of them into itself. It interacts with space, time, the author's biographical makeup, and construction of the main characters in what is arguably a more complex and more comprehensive system than the way in which a symbol, image, or metaphor operates in a literary work. The chronotope may be an abstract, overarching concept, a physical place, and the intersection of space and time, but all of these things are activated only through the consciousness of the individual in his or her lived time. Again, the "intersection of axes and fusion of [temporal and spatial] indicators" ("Forms of Time and the Chronotype in the Novel" 84) establishes the chronotope as multileveled and meaning laden.

Later in the same essay ("Forms of Time and the Chronotype in the Novel"), in a discussion of the Greek romance and the significance of travel through foreign countries, Bakhtin emphasizes what he calls "the author's own real homeland":

First and foremost, we have at the center of the travel novel's world the *author's own real homeland*, which serves as an organizing center for the point of view, the scales of comparison, the approaches and evaluations determining how alien countries and cultures are seen and understood. . . . In the novel of travel, this sense of a native country in itself—that is, as an internal organizing center for seeing and depicting what is located "at home"— radically changes the entire picture of a foreign world. . . . Furthermore, the hero in such a novel is . . . governed by his sociopolitical, philosophical, and utopian interests. In addition, the factor of the journey itself, the *itinerary*, is an actual one . . . finally, biography is the crucial organizing principle for time. ("Forms of Time and the Chronotype in the Novel" 103–4, emphasis original)

Indeed, Russia and the essential features of her culture function as the main organizing principle in the ruralist writers' literary corpus. Their ideas concerning Russia find a home in the major characters of their works, and both their own biographies (intrinsically linked with the tragedy endured by so many under Soviet rule) and those of the main characters form "the crucial organizing principle for time." A conceptual, psychological unity is created among the components of the writer's identity, his Russian patriotism, and the types of characters and literature that issue from a personal, specific identification with the general image of a loved and threatened homeland.

Thus Russia is a natural image for these writers. But how does one figure Russia as a chronotope? As I argue above, one productive way would be to locate this image within an available typology of "Russias of the mind," as expressed in ruralist literature. Parthé has developed such a typology in her recent scholarly work,[16] and she underscores:

There is a strong spatial aspect to the rhetoric of Russian national identity; reconstructing and studying the cognitive maps that Russians have drawn over the centuries provides a code of reading not just for cultural texts but also for the country's internal and external political behavior. . . . Russia is envisioned as a spiritually charged space filled by locations marking not gentle gradations along a spectrum of values, but sharp contrasts of sacred/ demonic, orthodox/heretical, Rus/NonRus. "Spiritual geography" and "spiritual borders" (terms found in Russian texts) map the sacred places, cultural and political, imaginary and real, providing a guide to a Russia that was and might be again.[17]

Parthé identifies five different cognitive maps linked with Russia that comprise the *"russkaia geografiia"* she discusses:[18]

1. *imperial*—includes "all lands where Russians live," and takes into itself the post-1991 "near abroad" (*blizhnee zarubezh'e*).
2. *spiritual*—embraces "all significant sacred places whether or not they are within Russia's borders, and whether they are real or imaginary. "Kiev, Kulikovo, Oblomovka, Kitezh, the Old Believer's promised land of Belovod'e, Constantinople, Jerusalem, and even Heaven and Hell are all superimposed on the national map, becoming part of the [multidimensional] spaces known as 'Russia.'"[19]
3. *symbolic*—links specific places in Russia with the whole of the country, associating the fate suffered by the particular with that endured by the entire country. Parthé notes, "one location . . . is seen as pure, unspoiled, even righteous, and it stands for the whole, not just figuratively, but in the very real sense that any harm or neglect this place suffers threatens the well-being of Russia itself."[20]
4. *regional/national(ist)* (my term—VZN)—relates to map 3 and "fore-grounds certain regions (Siberia, the North) or specific locations (Moscow, Irkutsk) as being more 'Russian' than others."[21]
5. *internal*—identifies "a spiritual map of Russia or Rus that is said to exist within all true Russians, no matter where they live. Like a traveling icon, it can go wherever a Russian is carried by fate, into war or exile."[22]

Parthé's typology provides discrete reference points that allow us to examine more clearly how Russia functions as a chronotope in ruralist writing. The works of Astafiev, Rasputin, and Soloukhin interact with Parthé's cognitive maps 2, 3, and 4 (2—spiritual, 3—symbolic, and 4—regional/national[ist]), but they conflate the spiritual map with the symbolic and the regional/national(ist). To be sure, both symbols and real places assume a spiritual significance in the context of village literature's concern for and veneration of Russia.

Astafiev's loosely structured chronicle of his return to his childhood home in Siberia near the northern Yenisei River employs various images and metaphors representative of the spiritual/geographical "map" of Russia and the country's fate, to wit: the dewdrop, the Turukhansk lily, the Queenfish, the town of Igarka, the "grandfather" river Yenisei, and the Siberian taiga. His description of the dewdrop (in the chapter titled "The Dewdrop") and the autobiographical main character's relationship to it while on a camping trip becomes an extended metaphor for everything that is spiritually important in Russia; the dewdrop also attains significance in the symbolic and regional/national(ist) cognitive maps above.

On the tapering tip of an oblong willow leaf, an oblong dewdrop collected, swelled into a clot of latent energy, and froze there lest it bring the world down with its fall.

I too froze.

. . . The willow leaf held [the dewdrop] in check in its groove, and the weight of the drop could not, at least not yet, overcome the resilient tenacity of the leaf. "Don't fall! Don't fall!" I entreated, I begged, I prayed, listening with my skin and my heart to the peace that abode in me and the world. (80–81)

Astafiev's dewdrop, poised to fall and "bring the world down," exists in the natural environment of his homeland Siberia, a region that in the novel symbolizes what is worth preserving, and what may be lost, in Russia. The regional map is spiritually and geographically contained within the national(ist) map of Russia.

Rasputin's "Farewell to Matyora" repeats these associations: the regional images of the island (the central one), its cemetary, the indestructible larch tree, and the "master" (*khoziain*) remain profoundly linked with Russia's most enduring traditions and with the main characters' (and author's) fears for the country's future. The island of Matyora intersects both space and time, and functions as a spiritual and geographical symbol of Russia:

Once more spring had come, one more in the never ending cycle, but for Matyora this spring would be the last, the last for both the island and the village that bore the same name. Once more, rumbling passionately, the ice broke, piling up mounds on the banks, and the liberated Angara River opened up, stretching out into a mighty, sparkling flow. . . . It all had happened many times before, and many times Matyora had been caught up in nature's changes. . . .

And so this year, too, the people planted their gardens. . . . [But] Matyora wasn't the same . . . [t]he roosters still sang out loudly, the cows bellowed, and the dogs barked noisily, but the village was fading, you could see that it had already faded: like a half-chopped tree, it had lost its roots, it was out of cycle. Everything was in place, but everything was wrong. . . . (*Farewell to Matyora* 1–2)

Distilled in this quotation are the most deeply felt concerns of the village writers about the vanishing way of life of Russia's past. One also notes in it the chronotopic function of Matyora—Rasputin's description focuses on a specific place undergoing radical, unalterable change—not the organic changes linked with cyclical time, but rather an interruption of the island's natural rhythms. The island takes on significance because of the aggregate of individual consciousnesses that have converged there and interacted meaningfully with each other for many generations. Again, in Bakhtin's terms, "[t]ime . . . thickens . . . [and] space becomes charged and responsive to the movements of time, plot, and history"

("Forms of Time and the Chronotype in the Novel" 84–85). The spatial and the temporal converge as the individual characters are caught up in this matrix of forces that suggests a microcosm of Russia. Moreover, Russia (symbolized by Matyora) is elevated to a spiritually significant level when the island and its various inhabitants (both flora and fauna) are described in mythical terms: the larch tree mysteriously defies all attempts to destroy it, the "master" patrols the island as an animal spirit, and the old man Bogodul evokes Russian folkloric "odd fellows" (*chudaki*) who are earthy and eccentric, but ultimately loyal to an established way of life.

Fred Davis, a sociologist of nostalgia, describes literature of memory as possessing a "distinctive, aesthetic modality" that "lacks a position in objective time."[23] Parthé points out that Davis "sees the time perspective as the characteristic that differentiates nostalgia from other forms of consciousness" (10). According to Davis:

> Unlike the "vivid present" of everyday life—that intersection of clock time and our inner time sense—nostalgia leaps backward into the past to rediscover and revere it. Here present clock time loses much of its relevance, and because the rediscovered past is clothed in beauty temporal boundaries are extended in imagination well beyond their actual chronological span. (80–81)[24]

Parthé and Davis help us to understand how the spatial and temporal aspects of the chronotope relate in particular to Village Prose, a body of writing linked with nostalgia. The spatial boundaries of Matyora are extended beyond their actual territory: Matyora becomes symbolic for all of Russia, and, indeed, Russia in this relationship functions chronotopically as the energizing, life-sustaining force that defines and contains the individual experiences and consciousnesses that in turn comprise the country's cultural and mythological identities. It is worth emphasizing here that myths are linked with a perceived reality: they derive from a people's attempt to understand the world, and subsequently to define and reconceptualize for itself that arrived-at understanding.

Both Astafiev and Rasputin frame their respective narratives with questions they pose, to themselves and their readers, in the spirit of Gogol's well-known lines at the end of *Dead Souls, I* ("Rus! Where are you going? Answer me. . . . No answer."). In *Farewell to Matyora* Rasputin ponders the meaning of life through the main character Darya, whose moral qualities he foregrounds as a shining example of Russia's peasant women:[25]

> And Darya still questioned herself, still tried to answer and couldn't answer. And who could? Man comes into the world, lives, and then when he's tired

of life like Darya or when he's not, inevitably goes back. How many there were that came before her, and how many more there'll be after! . . . And who knows the truth about man, why he lives? For the sake of life itself, the sake of children, so that his children leave children . . . or for the sake of something else? Would this movement be eternal? . . . Here they [graves] lie in full Matyora array, silent, hundreds of them who gave up their all for her, for Darya. . . . What should a person feel for whom hundreds of generations have lived? He feels nothing. He understands nothing. And he behaves as though life began with him and will end with him forever. (180)

Astafiev leaves the question hanging in the last chapter of *Queenfish*, "No Answer For Me":

My native Siberia has altered. Everything flows, everything changes, everything testifies to the hoary wisdom of the ages. Thus it was. Thus it is. Thus it shall be.
    To every thing there is a season, and a time to every purpose under the heavens. . . . [the verses from Ecclesiastes 3:1–8 appear in toto]
    So what have I been seeking? Why torment myself?
    Why? Why?
    No answer for me. (443–44)

The implied answer speaks volumes to us: clearly Astafiev is tormented by the question of moral and ethical answerability, but how? and for what? Throughout its pages *Queenfish* is constructed around the "actually performed act"—the courageous translation of a thought into its accompanying action. What Astafiev achieves in the depiction of the novel's major characters (for example, the autobiographical narrator/character and Akim) is reminiscent of Bakhtin's elaboration of the relationship between the act and the "ongoing event" (event approaching its completion):

. . . he sees clearly *these* individual, unique persons whom he loves, *this* sky and *this* earth and *these* trees . . . and what is also given to him simultaneously is the value, the actually and concretely affirmed value of these persons and these objects . . . and he understands the ought of his performed act, that is, *not* the abstract law of his act, but the actual, concrete ought conditioned by his unique place in the given context of the ongoing event." (*TPA* 30, emphasis original)

Bakhtin continues, "An emotional-volitional tone is an inalienable moment of the actually performed act . . . insofar as it is really actualized in Being, becomes a participant in the ongoing event" (*TPA* 33). The ethical standards of Astafiev's characters in *Queenfish* are made manifest both through their thoughts and their "actually performed acts," which concretely realize their thoughts and clarify without a doubt their full participation in Being.

As I note earlier in this essay, Soloukhin's case is somewhat marked: he shares the concerns voiced by Astafiev and Rasputin about Russia's fate, but his emphasis differs from theirs. In his poetic cycle "To My Friends" he attempts a rehistoricizing of Russia's past, especially of the Civil War period and the 1920s in the light of Lenin's policies. The cycle's following salient quatrains (from the poem also titled "To My Friends") articulate Soloukhin's perspective, one that reminds us, again, of the three cognitive maps of Russia:

> Russia has not yet perished,
> My friends, we're still around.
> Graves, graves, graves—
> Impossible to count. (stanza 1)
> . . . .
> Russia is shrouded in darkness,
> Russia is one common mound—
> However, she has not perished,
> Because, friends, we're still around.
>
> Hold on and build up your strength,
> Heed the message that she sends.
> Russia will not perish
> As long as we're here, my friends! (stanzas 17–18—last two)[26]

Soloukhin and those who share his views participate in the drama of saving Russia from her enemies, whether real or imagined. This is their acknowledged mission, and in this context their writing becomes sacramental: the poem and the cycle suggest a pact among the Russian patriots to defend Russia. Whereas Astafiev and Rasputin do not move beyond a detailed description of individuals in specific geographical places who question the morality of artifically induced, catastrophic changes, Soloukhin's rhetorical position explicitly locates answerability— and complicity ("Heed the message that she sends. / Russian will not perish / As long as we're here, my friends!")—in the participating and observing individual. For Soloukhin, as for Astafiev and Rasputin, the performed aesthetic act indeed "constitutes a going out *once and for all* from within possibility . . . into *what is once-occurrent*" (*TPA*, 28–29): the event of the literary work.

The preceding examples from Astafiev, Rasputin, and Soloukhin clearly locate the writers' work within Parthé's spiritual, symbolic, and regional/national(ist)

cognitive maps of Russia. Concrete geographical places (near the Yenisei and
Angara rivers) and powerful symbols (the dewdrop, the island Matyora, and the
"grave" of Russia) are foregrounded as part of a larger body of writing (Village
Prose) and, I might add, even larger philosophical canon on the "Russian idea" and
the meaning of Russia.[27]

Ultimately, it is Bakhtin's concept of answerability that shapes the aesthetic responses of Astafiev, Rasputin, and Soloukhin to the rapidly changing phenomenon
we call contemporary Russian culture and society. Bakhtin states in "Art and Answerability":

> When a human being is in art, he is not in life, and conversely. There is no
> unity between them and no inner interpenetration within the unity of an
> individual person.
>   But what guarantees the inner connection of the constituent elements
> of a person? Only the unity of answerability. I have to answer with my own
> life for what I have experienced and understood in art, so that everything I
> have experienced and understood would not remain ineffectual in my life.
> But answerability entails guilt, or liability to blame. It is not only mutual
> answerability that art and life must assume, but also mutual liability to blame.
>   . . . it is certainly easier to create without answering for life, and easier
> to live without any consideration for art.
>   Art and life are not one, but they must become united in myself—in
> the unity of my answerability. (1–2)

It is this notion of answerability that the ruralist writers incorporate into their
writing in both explicit and implicit ways: because they embed their personal views
on Russia in their creative work as a matter of conscience, these philosophical and
moral convictions form a vibrant part of the fabric of their literature.
    Both Bakhtin and the ruralist writers reject the separation of life from art;
in this context one is reminded of Nikolai Berdyaev's comment in his *The Origin
of Russian Communism*: "Russian writers with unusual acuteness lived through the
tragedy of creative power faced by the imperative need to transform life itself, to
bring truth into actual expression" (77–78).[28] Furthermore, Bakhtin in his complex
ethics rejects pure theoretism as a moral approach to life and art;[29] Mihailovic
interprets Bakhtin's uneasiness with theoretism in the following terms:

> [t]wo approaches to knowledge have predominated in the worlds of learn-
> ing and the arts, theoretism or theoretical cognition (*teoretizm; teoreticheskoe
> poznanie*) and aestheticism. While this dichotomy may be valid as an epis-

temological point of departure, if strictly enforced and if each category is overcultivated to the point of monstrous overdevelopment, they result in a fundamentally passive attitude (*passivnost'*) toward values in a culture. (63–64)

Mihailovic points out that in "Toward a Philosophy of the Act"

Bakhtin states that the disembodied and unconcerned subject [*dlia razvo-ploshchennogo i bezuchastnogo sub"ekta*] is someone to whom all deaths *could be* of equal or commensurable significance . . . [Bakhtin] asserts that the use of theoretical thought is perfectly justifiable as long as it is relegated to the service function of providing a "technical moment" leading to a higher form of knowing and is not perceived as an epistemological *summa* in itself . . . to linger impassively on that purview of pure form . . . results in emptiness and moral indifference. (63; emphasis original)

The artist must take a stand and must resist becoming the "disembodied and unconcerned subject," must "mount the parapet," in Soloukhin's words, and express his or her convictions in literary or publicistic form:

> When Russia was captured
> And condemned to destruction,
> Not everyone betrayed her,
> Not everyone was a traitor. (stanza 1)
> . . . .
> I rise up, as on a parapet,
> Amidst the cowards and the boors.
> I don't need tears, I don't need sadness—
> Because it's my turn now, today![30]

Soloukhin's sharply worded sentiments evoke Bakhtin's moving statement many years earlier: "It is only my non-alibi in Being that transforms an empty possibility into an actual answerable act or deed . . ." (*TPA* 42).

The image of Russia (extending back in history to the period of medieval Rus) and the geographical places that comprise the country's territory have been a significant feature of Russian literature from the time of *The Lay of Igor's Host* (*Slovo o polku Igoreve*) to the present day. From Pushkin's St. Petersburg to Astafiev's Ugarka, Rasputin's Angara, and Soloukhin's Olepino, Russia's real places have become places of the mind and emotionally and politically charged settings for literary works. The works I have touched upon here in my discussion of answerability, the act, and the chronotope thus follow a well-established pattern of signification. I hope that my investigation of Russia in the context of Bakhtin's moral philosophy and literary theory will enable others to situate ruralist writing more accurately within this rich and sometimes controversial national literary tradition.[31]

Notes

I presented an earlier version of this essay at the national conference of the American Association of Teachers of Slavic and East European Languages on December 29, 1997 in Toronto, Canada.

1. In many places in this essay I use the term "ruralist writers," rather than "Village Prose writers" (the better-known designation) only in the interest of precision, since the essay also includes a discussion of poetry by a Village Prose writer, Vladimir Soloukhin. Although both terms appear in the essay, I deliberately choose "ruralist" when I have in mind both the prose works and poetry under consideration; elsewhere, the more general term "Village Prose" suffices.

2. I use the following editions of the ruralist literary works under consideration here: Viktor Astafiev, *Queenfish*, trans. Kathleen Cook, Katharine Judelson, Yuri Nemetski, Keith Hammond, and Angelia Graf (Moscow: Progress Publishers, 1982); Valentin Rasputin, *Farewell to Matyora*, trans. Antonina Bouis (1979; Evanston, Ill.: Northwestern University Press, 1991); and Vladimir Soloukhin, "To My Friends," trans. Alexandra Kostina (*Asheville Poetry Review*, vol. 4, no. 1, fall/winter 1997), 148–50.

3. M. M. Bakhtin, "Art and Answerability," in *Art and Answerability: Early Philosophical Essays by M. M. Bakhtin*, ed. Michael Holquist and Vadim Liapunov, trans. and notes Vadim Liapunov (Austin: University of Texas Press, 1990), 1–3; M. M. Bakhtin, *Toward a Philosophy of the Act*, trans. Vadim Liapunov, ed. Michael Holquist and Vadim Liapunov (Austin: University of Texas Press, 1993); Mikhail Bakhtin, "Forms of Time and of the Chronotope in the Novel: Notes toward a Historical Poetics," in *The Dialogic Imagination: Four Essays by M. M. Bakhtin*, ed. Michael Holquist, trans. Caryl Emerson and Michael Holquist (Austin: University of Texas Press, 1981), 84–258. In this essay I use the following abbreviations for the Bakhtin works I cite: "*TPA*" ("Toward a Philosophy of the Act"), and "*FTCN*" ("Forms of Time and the Chronotope in the Novel").

4. Alexander Mihailovic also links Bakhtin's early philosophical works with his conceptualization of the chronotope in his *Corporeal Words: Mikhail Bakhtin's Theology of Discourse* (Evanston, Ill.: Northwestern University Press, 1997), 44–48.

5. G. A. Tsvetov, *Russkaia derevenskaia proza. Evoliutsiia. Zhanry. Geroi* (St. Petersburg: Templan, 1992), 34 (translation mine). See also 23–40. In his *The Faces of Contemporary Russian Nationalism* (Princeton: Princeton University Press, 1983), John B. Dunlop concludes, "[o]ver the past two decades, the *derevenshchiki* [Village

Prose writers], as well as other nationalist cultural activists, have been attempting, consciously or unconsciously, to carry out a quiet revolution aimed at changing the attitudes of their countrymen" (111). See also 110–21.

6. Lisa Eckstrom, "Moral Perception and the Chronotope: The Case of Henry James," in *Bakhtin in Contexts: Across the Disciplines*, ed. Amy Mandelker (Evanston, Ill.: Northwestern University Press, 1995), 99–116.

7. Interestingly, this same patriotic response (as a deeply felt "individually answerable act") manifested itself in the form of philosophical writing by Russian emigrés of the first wave of emigration. See Nicolas Berdyaev's *The Russian Idea*, tr. R. M. French (Boston: Beacon Press, 1962) and Ivan Ilyin's *Nashi Zadachi* (Paris: Russkii obshche-voinskii soiuz, 1956), Vol. 1 (for example, 269–80 on Russian nationalism).

8. Gary Saul Morson, "Prosaic Bakhtin: *Landmarks*, Anti-Intelligentsialism, and the Russian Countertradition," in Mandelker, ed., *Bakhtin in Contexts: Across the Disciplines*, 33–78.

9. See Kathleen F. Parthé, *Russian Village Prose: The Radiant Past* (Princeton: Princeton University Press, 1992), 10, 25, 80, 109. On Village Prose and the chronotope, see *Russian Village Prose* 22–28, and Katerina Clark, "Political History and Literary Chronotope: Some Soviet Case Studies," in *Literature and History: Theoretical Problems and Russian Case Studies*, ed. Gary Saul Morson (Stanford: Stanford University Press, 1986), 230–46.

10. See Dmitrii Likhachev, *Zametki o russkom* (Moscow: Sovetskaia Rossiia, 1981), 61–70. The book appears in English translation as *Reflections on Russia* (Boulder: Westview, 1991), trans. Christina Sever, ed. Nicolai N. Petro.

11. See Dunlop, *The Faces of Contemporary Russian Nationalism*, 242–54 and 262–65 on the *vozrozhdentsy*; my article "Reinterpreting the Soviet Period of Russian History: Vladimir Soloukhin's Poetic Cycle *Druz'iam*," *Slavic and East European Journal*, 41, no. 1 (spring 1997): 74–93; and Parthe, *Russian Village Prose*.

12. Parthé, *Russian Village Prose*, 94–95.

13. Vladimir Ovechkin's *District Routine* (Raionnye budni, 1952) and Vladimir Soloukhin's *Vladimir Country Roads* (Vladimirskie proselki, 1957).

14. My essay does not imply that Village Prose cannot be linked (in its chronotopic, as well as other, aspects) with Socialist Realist prose. See Katerina Clark's fine study, *The Soviet Novel: History as Ritual* (Chicago: University of Chicago Press, 1981), in which she writes: "Recent Soviet fiction (and much unofficial writing) grew out of, rather than away from, the traditions that preceded it. . . . Even when writers advocate values they believe to be opposed to Stalinist values, they often articulate them against the old patterns" (236). Rather, this essay establishes the affinity Bakhtin felt for nineteenth-century literature as based on the same literary qualities one can observe in Village Prose.

15. See Jay Ladin, "Fleshing Out the Chronotope," in Caryl Emerson, ed.,

Critical Essays on Mikhail Bakhtin (New York: G. K. Hall and Co., 1999), 212–36. Ladin's article offers an exciting direction for future investigations into the chronotope. My work in the present essay, however, relies instead on Parthé's cognitive typology, in part out of my concern (similar to Ladin's) for the need to provide a viable framework for a discussion of the concepts of the chronotope, answerability, and act, and in part because of the typology's clear relevance to Village Prose and issues of Russian patriotism.

16. Parthé, "The 'Geography' of Russian Identity During the Stalinist Years," unpublished conference paper; and "Russia's 'Unreal Estate': Cognitive Mapping and National Identity" (Kennan Institute for Advanced Russian Studies, Occasional Paper 265).

17. Parthé, "The 'Geography' of Russian Identity . . . ," 1. The connection between Russian national identity and geography has been made by many thinkers, among them Berdyaev and Likhachev. In his *The Russian Idea* Berdyaev describes a "spiritual geography" (*dukhovnaia geografiia*) on 2 (also cited in Parthé's "Russia's 'Unreal Estate' . . . ," 20n8). In *Reflections on Russia* Likhachev notes: "I have already noted how strongly the Russian plain affects the character of the Russian people. In recent years we often forget the geographic factor in human history" (16). Like Likhachev, Berdyaev points out in *The Origin of Russian Communism* (Ann Arbor: University of Michigan Press, 1964): "The immensity of Russia, the absence of boundaries, was expressed in the structure of the Russian soul. The landscape of the Russian soul corresponds with the landscape of Russia, the same boundlessness, formlessness, reaching out into infinity, breadth" (9).

18. See Parthé, "The 'Geography' of Russian Identity . . . ," 1–3. I paraphrase and include brief quotes from the five maps on 1–3, and recast map 4 slightly.

19. Ibid., 3.

20. Ibid., 4.

21. Ibid., 5.

22. Ibid., 5.

23. Fred Davis, *Yearning for Yesterday: A Sociology of Nostalgia* (New York: Free Press/Macmillan, 1979), 73, 77. Also cited in Parthé, *Russian Village Prose* 10.

24. Also cited in Parthé, *Russian Village Prose* 10. Davis's description of a beautiful, revered past whose temporal boundaries extend into the present by means of the imagination evokes Bakhtin's characterization of the epic: "In the past, everything is good: all the really good things (i.e., the "first" things) occur *only* in this past. The epic absolute past is the single source and beginning of everything good for all later times as well" (Mikhail Bakhtin, "Epic and Novel," in *The Dialogic Imagination: Four Essays by M. M. Bakhtin*), 15; emphasis original. I thank Anne Breznau for pointing out this connection to me.

25. One is reminded of the positive images of peasant women in Nikolai Nekrasov's long poem *Komu na Rusi zhit' khorosho* (Who is happy in Russia? written

1863–78) and Alexander Solzhenitsyn's story "Matrenin dvor" (Matryona's house, published in *Novyi mir*, January 1963).

26. Trans. Alexandra Kostina; originally published as "Druz'iam" in Vladimir Soloukhin, *Severnye berezy* (Moscow: Molodaia Gvardiia, 1990), 58–59.

27. See Nicolai N. Petro, *The Rebirth of Russian Democracy* (Cambridge: Harvard University Press, 1995), 88–111, 112–25 on the Russian Idea and the White Idea, respectively; and Catherine Andreyev, *Vlasov and the Russian Liberation Movement: Soviet Reality and Emigre Theories* (New York: Cambridge University Press, 1987).

28. Berdyaev, *The Origins of Russian Communism*, 77–78.

29. On Bakhtin's rejection of theoretism, see *TPA* 18–20, 28–30 and Mihailovic 62–65. In their *Mikhail Bakhtin: Creation of a Prosaics* (Stanford, Calif.: Stanford University Press, 1990), Gary Saul Morson and Caryl Emerson note, "In his earliest writings . . . Bakhtin faults theoretism for an error analogous to monologization. Those who understand ethics in terms of rules make a mistake similar to the understanding of language in terms of codes. They assume that it is possible to 'transcribe' an event so as not to lose its essential features, but in so doing, the event loses all the singularity from which responsibility derives" (58–59). See also Morson, "Prosaic Bakhtin: *Landmarks*, Anti-Intelligentsialism, and the Russian Countertradition," in Mandelker, *Bakhtin in Contexts: Across the Disciplines*," esp. 58–63.

30. From Soloukhin's poem "Nastala ochered' moia" (It's my turn now) in "Druz'iam," published in *Severnye berezy*, 60–61. Translation mine.

31. I would like to thank Gary Saul Morson for giving me the idea for this essay by noting in email correspondence that Russia in Village Prose could be richly analyzed as a chronotope. My gratitude also goes to the following readers of the essay: Anne Breznau, Gary Saul Morson, and Richard Nollan.

Contributors

David Krasner is an assistant professor of theater and the director of undergraduate theater studies at Yale University. He is the author of *Resistance, Parody, and Double Consciousness in African American Theatre, 1859–1910* and is editing *African American Theatre History and Performance Studies: A Critical Reader*. He is working on his next book, a history of African American theatre and performance from 1910 to 1930.

Kimberly A. Nance is an associate professor of Spanish and the director of graduate studies in foreign languages at Illinois State University. Her articles on social protest narrative and folklore/literature relations have appeared in *Style, Hispanic Journal, Chasqui, Hispanófila,* and *Letras Femeninas,* and her current research concerns the production, reception, and potential of *testimonio* as a social project.

Valerie Z. Nollan is an associate professor of Russian and the chair of the Department of Modern Languages and Literatures at Rhodes College. Her translation of Vladimir Soloukhin's *A Time to Gather Stones* was published in 1993 by Northwestern University Press, and her articles on twentieth-century Russian literature have appeared in *Russian Language Journal, Slavic and East European Journal,* and *Kontinent.* Her current project is a translation into English of Vladimir Solovyov's *Philosophical Principles of Integral Knowledge.*

Jacqueline A. Zubeck is a visiting assistant professor of English at Manhattan College in New York; her doctoral dissertation is titled "Murder in the Name of Theory: Theoretical Paradigms and Ethical Problems in Works by Dostoevsky, Gide, and DeLillo." Her research interests involve nineteenth- and twentieth-century fiction, particularly the work of Dostoevsky and Don DeLillo.